Vegan Ramayana

The Shakahara StarFire
Way of Rama

By Teja Shankara

Vegan Ramayana: The Shakahara StarFire Way of Rama

A former version was published by Teja Shankara in 2019, entitled *The Tejaswini Ramayana: The Way of Rama in the Shakahara StarFire Universes*.

Printed & distributed by Lulu, Inc., www.lulu.com

ISBN 978-1-300-76768-8

For the animals

(And for the human animals,
May we have compassion for
the non-human animals,
who are brothers and sisters
in our earthling family.)

Contents

Why "Vegan" Ramayana?

In my book *The Tejaswini Ramayana: The Way of Rama in the Shakahara StarFire Universes*, I neglected to clearly explain *why* I felt inspired to write my own version of the ancient Indian epic. There are more than three hundred recorded Ramayanas, and I have studied more than a dozen versions because I fell in love with the story and the spiritual states it activates in my being. Immersed in the tale I felt elevated, and yet I also felt pained by reading so many non-vegan aspects within one of the world's most holy scriptures. Those aspects were not in alignment with the highest Vedic principle of doing no harm (ahimsa).

There are no perfectly pure vegans, but each vegan strives to do as little harm as possible on their ever-evolving vegan journey. At a certain stage in my journey, I could no longer tolerate reading about or hearing others talking about eating dairy, cooking meat, and so on. I felt like I was complying just simply by reading or hearing, so I developed habits such as: when reading, I would cross out non-vegan things and write "Sorry, animals" and when hearing, I would look down in silence, because in many situations it would not be socially appropriate to speak out. It would not change people's minds and it would cause alienation.

So this issue of complicity, that many vegans face, often compelled me to write "Sorry, cows" in the margins of the earlier versions of the Ramayana. It is painful to feel so much compassion for the animals while living in such a non-vegan world which advertises meat and dairy in all directions. Thus I decided to veganize the Ramayana so people could at least take peaceful refuge in a sacred text that is non-violent.

I believe that spiritual texts and leaders should be scrutinized and updated. For example, in this vegan version, through Sita's love transmission Sri Rama and Brother Lakshmana suddenly loved all the animals even more than they had already loved them, so they could never again be hunters like they were in earlier versions.

Several thousand years after Rama and Sita's time in India, another avatar graced planet Earth with a similar love for all creatures — Jesus Christ. He was enraged by the sales and killings of animals in the temple... So then why would he eat his fish brothers? Did he actually eat fish, or was that fabricated by later biblical writers?

Then, in the thirteenth century, Saint Francis deeply loved all living creatures, and preached to them as though they had souls just like humans. He endearingly called the feathered beings "sister birds"... So then why would he eat whatever was placed before him? Apparently he said that the Holy Gospel instructed people to eat whatever was placed before them. That seems inconsistent with his love for all the animals. Did he actually eat meat, or was that invented by later Franciscan writers?

Then, in 2007, Zen Buddhist Master Thich Nhat Hanh announced that his monasteries would shift to the vegan diet to help the environment, and he spoke out publicly about not harming the animals... So then why did his nuns recently share a video in which they made lemon honey as medicine? Perhaps they do not know that stealing honey harms the bees.

And, Native Americans honor the Great Spirit within all beings... So then why do many of them still eat dead animals? They say that the animals offer themselves willingly (and are honored as sacred through rituals), but that is a projection from the human mind. The reality is the animals want to live. The humans have well-meaning intentions with their projected ideas, but those ideas are actually coming from the shadow side. It is the dark side of their egos convincing them that it is okay to kill their brother and sister animals. There is no "humane" killing.

Similar to the Native Americans, the Tibetan Buddhists also live very much connected to nature... So then why do they drink butter tea? Again, it is the shadow side convincing them that it is okay to steal fluids from animals.

There are many other examples of good intentions which are actually shadow, such as "free range" and "grass fed" meats. In the Holocaust, if the Nazis had given the Jews nice accommodations and good food, then would it have been okay to slaughter them?

By the way, when people use the term "Vegan Nazis" that is the ultimate irony — that is total projection and gaslighting. The vegans are the ones who want to stop the insane massive killing of other beings, so they are definitely not the people to be called Nazis! In reality, the Nazis are the people who participate in killing animals, either directly or indirectly.

Getting back to India, Sri Rama was the seventh avatar of Lord Vishnu, born about seven thousand years ago, and the next avatar, Sri Krishna, was born about five thousand years ago. Krishna ate dairy, and his followers today have not updated their ahimsa practice to meet the current conditions, and so the cows who they adore are suffering horribly. That is a painful irony.

Any guru who gives out thousands and thousands of cows' *milk* chocolates yearly should be questioned. But, the devotees insist that they cannot question the actions of their guru. That is wrong. We each have to find the truth inside ourselves and not listen to anyone else, not even a living avatar.

The utmost respect and love for a cow is to let her live her natural life and feed her own calves. Unfortunately, some unnatural traditions have gotten deeply ingrained, but they can be changed. Even if something has been done for generations, that does not mean it is right.

The cows are living breathing beings who do not want to be eaten, nor do they want to share their milk with other species. They want to live in freedom with their families just like humans. By nature, their milk is intended for their own calves — it is not for humans. Each species makes milk for its own species to thrive on. No species makes milk for another species.

When anyone says that the cows happily give their milk to humans, that is projection. The people who say such untruths are simply projecting what they wish to believe, based on the brainwashing they have received from religions and from the dairy industry — and also based on their addiction to the fat in the dairy. But, the truth will be found deep in meditation. Compassion for all beings arises naturally in meditation, at different times for different people.

Some Indian swamis (spiritual teachers) say that they are pretty much vegan, but they drink "ahimsa milk" which they claim the cows lovingly give to them after first feeding their own calves. This voluntary gift of "leftover milk" *idea* seems totally absurd. Again, it is a projection of human ideas. In reality, each cow makes the milk for her own precious calf.

The highest Vedic principle, ahimsa, doing no harm, means vegan. It means no more ghee ever again! It means pour some holy coconut oil over the puja fire instead. It means bow down to all of those suffering holy cows and beg their forgiveness.

I think that Hinduism needs to look at the ahimsa doctrine with fresh eyes and be open to some serious updating. Perhaps five thousand years ago the people and cows lived together harmoniously (although that is questionable), but that is certainly not the reality of today's dairy cows who are enduring horrific lives.

In order for humans to indulge in cow secretions, commonly referred to as milk and dairy products, the baby calves are taken away from their mommas. Both the babies and the mothers grieve this incredibly unnatural separation. The momma cows are forcibly impregnated again and again in a painful procedure done by human beings who should never have to perform such disgusting work. Many male calves are slaughtered to be sold as a meat called veal, and after the mother cows stop producing milk, they are killed to be hamburgers and steaks for human consumption. The entire dairy operation is unbelievably weird, unnatural, and inhumane.

Cows are sentient beings, which means that they are aware and able to feel pain and pleasure through their senses. Cows are conscious of their surroundings and their relationships. They experience both physical and psychological pain, caused by the humans who exploit and abuse them.

Doing no harm would mean giving up all animal products, including meat, fish, honey, and eggs. And it would mean giving up all dairy products including ghee, butter, yogurt, milk, cheese, and ice cream.

After ten thousand years of animal agriculture, humankind has been thoroughly brainwashed to believe that it is natural and necessary to eat the flesh and fluids of living, feeling beings. This massive global brainwashing has caused human beings to fiercely defend their addictions to eating meat, fish, dairy, and eggs, even though the research clearly shows that animal products cause many illnesses, including heart disease, diabetes, cancer, obesity, and so on.

(For information about the connection between veganism and optimal health, visit **pcrm.org**, the website for the Physicians Committee for Responsible Medicine, whose President, Neal Barnard, MD, writes that the vegan diet is a powerful tool to prevent, manage, and even reverse diabetes. Additional vegan resources include **forksoverknives.com** and **drmcdougall.com**.)

The animals who are farmed as commodities, such as cows, pigs, lambs, chickens, turkeys, and fish, are precious living beings who have families and *feelings* just like cats, dogs, and humans. They all want to live in freedom.

In the Ramayana, when Sita asked Rama to catch the golden deer to be her playmate, Rama said that her desire to possess it was understandable. Certainly, there exists a human inclination to keep animals as pets, but that does not make it right. Most vegans agree that it is wrong to keep animals in zoos, circuses, rodeos, races, laboratories, and so on, but they keep dogs and cats as pets (and have to buy meat to feed those pets). Most vegans have not yet begun to question the pet phenomenon, but there is a fringe group of us who think that we should find ways to compassionately phase it out. We should help the ones who need help in sanctuaries, but stop breeding and stop keeping them in private homes.

The pets, commonly referred to now as "companion animals" and "fur babies," are said to help humans in many ways, such as with depression and loneliness, but we should encourage humans to help other humans, and let the animals live in the freedom that is their birthright, same as ours.

Humankind needs to realize the truth so aptly put by my fellow pet-free vegan friend, Shankar Narayan: "Cow is not your mother, puppy is not your baby. You have your own family and they have theirs too. Respect this and let them live their lives."

The Ramayana is a potent tool for coping with grief. One of the main themes of the epic is the pain of separations. This motif is relatable for most people who are engaged in the predicaments of the human condition: we want to love and be loved, but then the inevitable separations cause us terrible pain.

In contemplating this, we can then think of the painful separations which billions of non-human animals are *needlessly* forced to endure each year for the satisfaction of humans. Those separations are unnatural; they are *not* inevitable; they are not kind; and they are not ahimsa — they cause harm.

In the version of Ramayana by Kamala Subramaniam, when Hanuman brought Sita's ornament across the sea, Rama said, "Seeing this jewel my mind is sorely distressed as a mother cow's will, when it thinks of her calf." ("It" should be "she" because cows are living beings, not things. Language matters!) In that statement Rama illustrated the truth that modern scientists are discovering: a mother cow has a mind which *thinks* of her calf. As previously stated, cows experience emotional pain when separated from their loved ones. They may not think in words like humans, but they definitely *feel* emotions.

Another example: later in that same text, Rama asked, "How can I comfort them who will weep like mother deer who have been parted from their young?" (*Ramayana* by Kamala Subramaniam, Bharatiya Vidya Bhavan, Mumbai, India, 1981.)

In some earlier versions of the Ramayana they performed rituals with animal sacrifices, like of horses and deer. There was a custom of killing and cooking a deer for a ritual called "Vastu Shanti." Well, 'shanti' means 'peace' and in that custom there was no peace for the killed deer. That scene did not make sense because otherwise Rama deeply loved the peaceful deer and they loved him. Also, Rama repeatedly said that violence was wrong. And, in ancient India many people believed that it was a sin to kill a cow and it was also a sin to enjoy hurting animals.

The demons in the Ramayana ate human flesh. That illustrates how humans eating the flesh of animals puts humans on the cruel level of self-indulging carnivorous demons. Eating animals does not put humans on the level of divine kindness and mercy.

Vegetarianism is not enough to raise humanity to a higher level because most vegetarians eat dairy and eggs. As already explained, the dairy industry causes incredible suffering for the cows. And, in order for humans to eat the secretions of hens (eggs), the chickens also endure unbelievable, horrific suffering. The females are forced to lay an unnaturally high number of eggs in crowded filthy cages. And, whereas the male calves are slaughtered to be veal meat, the male chicks are often thrown into the garbage, sometimes alive.

Eating a vegan diet is best for the humans, and it is best for the Earth, and it is quite certainly best for the animals! When humans kill animals (for meat and fish) or steal from animals (for milk, butter, ghee, cheese, yogurt, eggs, and honey), the animals suffer tremendously. They feel fear and anger and sadness, and those low emotional vibrations continue to resonate in their flesh and fluids, which then go into the human body.

Conversely, plant foods carry clean, high vibrations into the human body. In this book I suggest coconut instead of dairy because the coconut is a sacred fruit in India and it is adored throughout the world. Take the bells off the holy cows and use the beloved fruits from within the holy coconut shells! (In reality, vegans can consume any dairy substitutes they like best, such as oat, rice, or hemp alternative plant "milks.")

Some people defensively argue that vegans are "killing" plants. Well, I cannot claim to know whether or not plants feel, but certainly they do not have brains and central nervous systems, so carrots do not scream when chopped like pigs scream when killed. We know that killing animals and fish causes incredible suffering, and stealing from cows, goats, chickens, and bees causes incredible suffering, but we really do not know if plants feel pain. And, we have to eat something to survive in these bodies.

The diet should be as compassionate as possible, and so at this stage in our evolution that means eating plants. But, who knows what the future will bring. Perhaps if all the human beings get elevated to the Highest Love Vibrations, then we will all live on Sunlight and vibrations from crystals! For now I say let's honor the plants and eat them with gratitude.

Visualizing humankind living on the frequencies of our beloved Sun star brings delight to the mind, even if it is quite fantastical. Fantasy is actually a gateway to peace. While being absorbed in a fantasy realm, such as this vegan version of

Ramayana, you can temporarily feel inner peace and feel right with the world. Then, after reading, you can bring that peaceful energy back to your reality.

The ancient tale of Ramayana already contains many fantastical elements such as animals talking and celestial beings showering flowers down upon earthlings. Many of the older versions described ships of the skies, which seem very much like UFOs, and the Lords Shiva, Vishnu, and Rama all have *blue* skin. They incarnate as avatars from beyond this terrestrial realm. So, in this version I added further science fiction elements to merge my love of Star Wars and my love of fantasy with the sacred science fiction aspects already depicted in the ancient versions of Ramayana.

Although I graduated college with a Political Science degree, as a spiritual visionary I admit that I can be a bit of a nonrealistic dreamer. But, 2020 shattered the self-created fantasy world that I had been living in for many years. My existence had sparkled with the glitter of an alternate reality, composed of New Age beliefs, stories, visions, and projections. The virus pandemic and its many ramifications catapulted me back into the shocking realities of the "real world" and brought me to the conclusion that the human species may only survive for another hundred years or so.

If humankind only exists for a short time longer, then I realize that world peace and world veganism are not likely to happen, but I still think it is good to visualize the highest ideals and work towards them. Thus, in Book Seven and in the Epilogue I shared what I mystically know is *possible* even though I logically know that it is not probable.

Regardless of where we are heading on this planet, it is always super important to align with the Forces of Goodness and to try to make this wounded world a better place for ourselves and for any future generations. We have an ethical duty to try to reduce the suffering, now, wherever and whenever we can, for the happiness of our dear brothers and sisters, of the human species, *and* of *every living species* on Earth.

Inspired by Mahatma Gandhi-ji, Martin Luther King, Jr., Jesus Christ, Zen Buddhist Master Thich Nhat Hanh, Saint Francis, and other holy beings, I choose to live a vegan lifestyle according to the highest Vedic principle of ahimsa, which is the vow of non-violence and non-harming. I pray for justice, mercy, and freedom for all the animals, and I send waves of loving compassion to those who harm animals and to those who eat the flesh and fluids of animals.

I shifted to the vegan diet in 2009, but I grew up eating meat (and many other animal products), wearing leather, visiting zoos and circuses, owning pets, and buying products that were tested on animals, so I understand that culture, and I know how people are brainwashed to indulge in it and to become addicted to its habits. I was also programmed to not feel connected with the animals, but when I began a daily meditation practice I quickly developed an aversion to harming other beings, including all the non-human animals. While I know that I am not a perfect vegan, I continually strive to do better.

My Shakahara StarFire Tribe aspires to live in the highest vegan ahimsa. I welcome others to join me in right timing.

Shakaharini StarFire Teja Ray
July 2021

Welcome

to *Vegan Ramayana....*

Prologue

The Supreme Intelligence of all the universes, who is referred to as Maha~Vishnu, exists at his primary abode in a distant StarFire Universe, on a blue planet that emits blue crystal fire sparks. On that planet, which is called Vaikunta, this Supreme Being, Maha~Vishnu, also called Hari, lives amongst a tribe of Blue Light Beings and divides his energy into a trinity named Brahma, Vishnu, and Shiva.

From the StarFire Universes, Vishnu, also known as Narayana, preserves and protects multiple universes, and manifests in parallel incarnations as Rama in multiple locations and dimensions simultaneously. Through the Avatar of Rama, he is able to help Goodness to keep winning in the struggles between good and evil. And so the story of the Ramayana (the Way of Rama) is continually playing out in many universes and times and dimensions. There are more than three hundred recorded Ramayanas, although thousands or even millions of Ramayanas are ever vibrating through the spheres...

... That play of Ramayana had been going on for thousands of years, and yet, Vishnu, in his cosmic form at Vaikunta, his home base, suddenly saw that something more needed to be done. In particular, he was watching a small planet called Earth in a distant galaxy, and he was perplexed by the actions of the dominant race of beings there, a species called humans. On that planet, he had often incarnated as Rama in a country called India, where he had developed quite a large following of devotees, and the story had spread to other countries on the planet as well.

Studying the situation on that planet, he saw that even though the Avatar of Rama had inspired a group of humans to stay on the path of goodness, which kept the balance of good winning over evil, there was still a significant amount of evil growing on the planet, and not only that, but even the ones who were following the path of Rama were struggling immensely with the battle of good and evil within themselves. The path of Rama helped uplift them, but still they were continuously battling the lower human vibrations that controlled their minds. Even the ones who sincerely desired to be highly virtuous, even they still regularly succumbed to the lower vibrations. And because the earthlings were multiplying at a very fast rate, and the majority of humans were not on the path of Rama, the balance was tipping towards evil taking over. Something new needed to be done to save the human race and their planet Earth.

And so the Supreme Being determined that clearly a faster path to Goodness was needed. Right at the moment when Hari realized that, in his mind's eye he saw Lord Shiva, another aspect of the Supreme Intelligence, who is also called Hara, and who resides simultaneously on a StarFire blue-sparking planet called Kailash, and with his Goddess Parvati on a sacred mountain, also called Kailash, in India on planet Earth. As Lord Vishnu watched Lord Shiva, he saw that Shiva was creating a Plan for a faster path to Goodness. He was creating this Plan deep inside the mind of a Shakaharini StarFire human being on planet Earth.

For this Plan to manifest, a new Ramayana needed to play out on Earth. Thus, *Vegan Ramayana: The Shakahara StarFire Way of Rama* would feature Lord Vishnu incarnating as the Avatar Rama, and Goddess Lakshmi incarnating as his wife Sita, along with many simultaneous parallel incarnations of Lord Vishnu happening in the forms of birds, monkeys, bears, and humans. To assist with the Plan, Lord Shiva would also incarnate the eleventh sphere of his energies as the Avatar of Lord Hanuman. These incarnations would serve the Elevating Mission that was integral to the Plan that Shiva was creating in the Shakaharini's mind.

Shiva originally conceived the ancient story of Ramayana, and eons ago he chose a sage-crow named Kakabhushundi to be the first to narrate it, so the sage-crow told the tale to Vishnu's Eagle brother, Garuda, along with many, many other birds at a holy lake, where Shiva listened as a swan! Then Shiva told the sacred story to his consort, Parvati Devi, then later Rishi Valmiki composed the epic in 24,000 verses, then later Valmiki was reborn as Tulsidas, and he told it with four viewpoints, and then, as it traveled the globe in translations, a Shakaharini StarFire tribal being began to study various versions and Shiva inspired her to tell a new version of Rama beamed in from the Shakahara StarFire Universes.

Dear reader, you may be wondering why or how you have come to this story at this time. Up until now, your life has probably been a series of ups and downs, of joys and sorrows, of triumphs and defeats. You may be feeling fed up with the cycles of miseries and struggles, and deep inside, you may have this vague knowing that there must be a better way to live on this Earth. Daily the bad news seems to be taking over the good, and yet there is likely still a feeling of hope deep within you. It is that intuitive knowing that things could get better.

Welcome to *Vegan Ramayana*. As you read the Elevations, you may experience pleasant sensations, such as tingling, in your body or even around your body, particularly just above the top of your head. You may also begin to notice positive changes (subtle or dramatic) in your daily life, in terms of your thoughts, words, intentions, and actions. These sensations and changes are natural reactions to reading about spiritual elevations. Stay open and allow yourself to be elevated.

Om Sri Shakahari Ganesha!
Om Sri Shakaharini Saraswati!
Om Sri Shakahari Rama! Om Sri Shakaharini Sita!
Om Sri Shakahari Hanuman! Om Sri Shakahari Shiva!

Book One

Beamed Into Incarnations

OM.

I, Shakaharini StarFire Teja Ray, ever reverence the eight billion beings of the human species, along with the four hundred billion bird beings, the two billion cow beings, the twenty billion chicken beings, the three million whale beings, and the one million elephant beings. I bow to every living, breathing creature of the land, sea, and air, with deep respect. And I also reverence, with deep humility, the Holy Vedas, the Shastras, the Puranas, the Upanishads, the Hindu mystics, saints, sages, gurus, gods, goddesses, and the Radiant Supreme Reality, the Brahman.

I humbly acknowledge that I am a beginner-scholar. In my mere seventeen years of studying on the Hindu Yoga Path, I have only learned a few tiny drops of the Vast Ocean that is the Spiritual Knowledge of India. I hereby apologize for any errors in this text, and I humbly give thanks to Lord Shiva for all that is right and true.

I also reverence the Ramayana itself. I bow in full prostration to its ancient power and wisdom. I love this story deeply, and I intend to share my version with respect, and to bring to it the highest vibrations of love that I know are possible.

Many human beings claim to have seen UFOs and higher planetary beings, who they say are coming to save humanity and the Earth from self-destructing. The Blue Space Beings, who have been sighted by these humans, are emanations of the Supreme Being, and they are indeed keen to the idea of elevating humanity. Beyond the universe that Earth exists in, there are innumerable universes, the Shakahara StarFire Universes, and the Supreme Being resides there in the aspects of Vishnu and Shiva, and beams into human bodies on Earth when necessary. These incarnations bring extraterrestrial energies that link the Earth with the Shakahara StarFire Universes.

So now it is time to begin this version...

Somewhere, far, far away, out in a distant galaxy of Shakahara StarFire Universes, Lord Vishnu and Lord Shiva began to confer about the Plan for the Vegan Ramayana incarnations. Communicating telepathically between their home stars, Vaikunta and Kailash, they shared that they had each thoroughly re-studied all of the many ancient Ramayanas, and this time they saw the need to create better strategies for keeping the Avatars elevated.

In the past, each time Rama had incarnated, due to being in a human body, he was affected by the physiological effects of the hormones, chemicals, thoughts, feelings, and sensations arising in the body.

Hari and Hara recognized that this would happen again to a certain extent because it was the inevitable consequence of being in a human body; however, this time they devised a strategy for minimizing the forgetfulness of the Avatars. Each time they would forget who they were and start to identify with their human body-mind complexes, those lower vibrations in their brains would sound off an alarm in Shiva's Awareness and he would then quickly remind them that they were Avatars, thus elevating them to rise above the effects of their human bodies.

With that Plan thus set, they peered down into the holy City of Ayodhya, in Northern India, and into the Palace of King Dasaratha, where Rama typically takes human birth. As in past Ramayanas, the King was conducting a fire ceremony with the hope of fulfilling his desire for sons. After the priests had chanted the prescribed Vedic mantras, while pouring volumes of holy coconut oil into the sacred flames, a shining being arose from the fire and offered a golden bowl of sweet coconut milk for the three royal Queens to drink. After they consumed the Shri~Pala (fruit of Goddess Lakshmi), Vishnu and Shiva saw that the moment was ripe for beaming down the Avatars. Thus Vishnu divided some of his energies and beamed them into the human wombs.

In due time, the King's three wives gave birth to four sons, as follows: Kausalya birthed Rama, Kaikeyi birthed Bharata, and Sumitra birthed the twins Lakshmana and Shatrughna. While Mother Kausalya was alone in her chamber with her newborn Rama, he showed her his cosmic form, as Maha~Vishnu, the Radiant Supreme Reality. Gleaming like a wild blue lotus in sunlight, he had four arms and was radiating a blinding light in all directions. His mother was instantly elevated to a very high state of consciousness, but then she worried about what might happen if he showed that form to others, so she begged him to take the form of an innocent human infant, such that everyone could love and adore.

The four boys grew up in an atmosphere of Love, Love, Love, and more Love. Everyone in the entire kingdom adored them, and they enjoyed sporting about in the royal gardens. Rama and Lakshmana went everywhere together, while Bharata and Shatrughna were equally inseparable. The two pairs delighted in making mischief about the palace. Rama loved to tease a magical black crow who followed him on all of his childish pranks.

After the royal four celebrated their seventh birthday, they began their studies with the high sages out in the woods, in an ashram just beyond the gardens. The brothers excelled in spiritual and psychic sciences, and the rishis saw clearly that they were unearthly children. By keen inner vision the munis discerned the Lord's lilas, thus they kept quiet about what they saw in the young princes.

While learning to shoot bows and arrows, the boys intuitively felt that something was wrong, and, according to the Plan, Lord Shiva instantly became aware of that uneasy feeling in the Avatars. While the boys were alone one morning, Shiva appeared before them, standing near the beloved bull Nandi, and reminded them that they were incarnations from a blue-sparking planet out in the Shakahara StarFire Universes. He told them that even though the highest Vedic principle was ahimsa, which means to do no harm, the human species was still killing animals, demons, and even other humans, so for a while they should just play along and learn to use the bows and arrows. Shiva elevated their consciousness to a level beyond words. Thus they simply accepted that later on they would understand the full meaning of that encounter.

One day when the princes were twelve and three-fourths years old, a powerful sage named Vishwamitra arrived at the court of King Dasaratha. That particular spiritual teacher was a man of fire who was renowned in all the spheres for his potent Shakti (spiritual power). Everyone in the room had to squint to see, due to the glare of his radiance. The King bowed low before Vishwamitra, showed him to a respected seat, and with palms joined, told him that he would do anything the sage asked of him. After everyone in the court was seated, Vishwamitra boomed out his request in a voice that resounded through many worlds: "I ask that you send your son Rama with me for the destruction of the demons who are interrupting my forest sadhana (spiritual practices)."

King Dasaratha, beginning to sweat, answered in a voice of panic: "No, not my favorite son Rama! I will go with you myself, with my vast army, and we will destroy the demons for you. But do not ask for my Rama, for he is only a young child!"

Sage Vishwamitra, locking eyes with the King, said, "Well, I guess you will not fulfill your word to do anything I ask of you. A King who does not keep his word! Such will be the reputation of your Solar Dynasty from now on."

As the sage stood up to leave, the King's guru, Vasishtha, said, "Wait. Do not leave in such haste," and turning to the King, advised him thusly: "In this earthly realm, attachment to loved ones causes much grief and suffering. Everyone understands your deep attachment to Rama. We all feel this immensity of affection towards the child. And yet, there are deeper forces at work in our lives than we can understand. Probably Vishwamitra knows the deeper meaning for his request but will not share it with this audience. Even though you do not understand the reasons for his request, you can trust that your Rama will be ever protected by this man of fire, even as the sacred nectar of the gods is ever protected by the spinning wheel of fire, blades, and serpents. Know that this rishi can be trusted. Send Rama to the forest with him now. You will not regret it, and later you will understand why this has happened."

Bowing to his guru, the King called for Rama and Lakshmana. As tears welled up in the Queens' eyes, the young princes touched their mothers' feet, then touched their father's feet, and then promptly departed with the sage.

Everyone in the court sat stunned for the remainder of the day, until the King sent everyone to do their twilight prayers by the holy River Sarayu. As they bowed to the setting sun, they thought of how Rama had gone that very way, many hours earlier, when departing on the journey with the sage.

Indeed, Vishwamitra had led the princes to the river, and they had crossed into the forest before the day was done. Rama and Lakshmana had never been so far from the palace, and they greatly enjoyed the adventure. The sage taught them many things that night beside a crackling fire, and the next morning, after sending prayers of gratitude to the rising sun, they completed the journey to his hermitage. Walking barefoot, single-file, they kept silent and absorbed the many wonders of the trees, plants, birds, and stones.

In the quiet of the forest, Rama simultaneously felt a soothing peace and a great wildness stirring within him, which reminded him of something long ago and far away.

When they arrived at Vishwamitra's ashram, the sage's students were chanting mantras and tending the sacred fire. The boys enjoyed the familiar scene, although Rama sensed that danger was lurking about, and he wondered what was going to happen next.

Vishwamitra read Rama's thoughts, so he invited the princes to sit by the fire, and over a simple meal of roots and fruits, he explained many things: "By deep inner vision, I am able to read the stars, the elements, and the thought-forms of all beings, including rocks, crystals, trees, birds, elephants, and humans. I know that you sense the danger here, but there is no need for worry, because there is a grand design to everything that is happening. In deep meditation, Lord Shiva has shown me the entire Plan for all of the Ramayanas throughout time and space.

"In many past Ramayanas, the demons were disrupting my fire rituals, so I brought you two here to destroy those rakshasas, including Tataka and her sons Subahu and Maricha. In the past I taught you much about using the power of mantras with weaponry. However, Shiva has laid down a New Way for this Ramayana. This time I will still teach you potent mantras, but they will be used to elevate rather than to destroy.

"When the fierce, grotesque Tataka comes to pour sand and human skulls over my sacred fire, you two will elevate her consciousness and she will sit down beside me like a tamed tiger. Then you will also elevate Subahu, but when Maricha sneaks by, you will send him flying hundreds of miles into the sea, so that he can still play his important role later in the story."

Vishwamitra noticed the puzzled looks on the shining faces of Rama and Lakshmana. He smiled to himself as Lord

31

Shiva suddenly appeared on the scene. Once again Shiva spoke to the boys in a manner that they did not fully understand, but they accepted his words without question. He reminded them that they were incarnations of Vishnu, and simply said that they should follow every instruction given by Vishwamitra.

Shiva winked at the sage and silently disappeared into a shimmering craft that hovered above the ground and seemed strangely alive. The spaceship instantly dissolved into another dimension, and the boys sat enchanted by it all.

And so, as per the Plan, Vishwamitra began his fire ceremony, in which he would sit in silent meditation for several days while the boys stood guard. Everything transpired just as the sage had predicted. Using the powerful mantras for elevation, Rama and Lakshmana elevated Tataka and Subahu, who sat down in peaceful meditation near the sage. Next, Rama hurled Maricha out towards the distant sea, and the celestial beings, who were watching from all the realms, serenely smiled.

After Vishwamitra completed the ceremony, he told the boys that it was time for them to journey to Mithila, the kingdom of the great King Janaka. The princes had learned about that philosopher-sage-king in their studies, and they were very keen to meet him. The three walked quickly along the paths, stopping only for brief rests.

Along the way, Rama saw a large stone which was emitting a very powerful energy. Sage Vishwamitra explained that long ago the Sage Gautama had caught his wife Ahalya in the arms of the thunder god Indra (who was disguised as her husband Gautama), and that normally calm sage had lost his temper and cursed Ahalya to be turned into stone until Rama would come and touch her with his holy feet.

The child Rama felt amused by that tale, and he innocently touched his feet to the rock. To Rama's delight, the rock instantly transformed into a beautiful woman. Just then the sage Gautama appeared, and Rama spoke to him in a voice of wisdom beyond his years: "Forgive your wife. She has been purified through this ordeal and you two can now live a happy holy life as monk and nun together in your ashram." The sage forgave his wife, as Rama advised, and the saintly pair touched

Rama's glistening blue feet. Then, in silence they departed for their hermitage in the trees.

The trio continued on their way. The sage felt immensely pleased with the princes of the Solar Dynasty. The birds in the trees sensed the rishi's inner joy, and they sang out in a sweetness of tones that resonated through many lokas (worlds). As they drew near Mithila, the flowers looked more colorful, the sandalwood groves gave off a more incredible scent, and the sun appeared brighter. Rama and Lakshmana sensed that they were entering a magical realm, and the sage noticed their excitement.

When they entered the kingdom, the guards rushed them immediately into the warm presence of King Janaka. In his nourishing voice, he welcomed them to his court: "Finally you are here. Everything is ready. Shall we begin?" Vishwamitra chuckled as the boys did not understand the King's funny introduction. The rishi explained, "Lord Shiva has also given the Plans to King Janaka, so he is referring to the part of the Ramayana in which you, Rama, join the contest of the bow."

Still the boys did not know what was about to happen, and the sages greatly enjoyed the play. King Janaka offered them respected seats, touched their feet, and then spoke seriously, "Some years ago, I found a radiant baby girl in a furrow on my land. We named her Sita and have raised her as our princess. Shortly before I found her, the Blue Tribes of the Shakahara StarFire Universes had beamed her into the Earth. She possessed the powers of Goddess Lakshmi even as an infant.

"When she was quite small, she lifted the incredible bow of Shiva, as if it were a peacock feather! At that moment I decreed that she would only marry if her suitor could also lift Shiva's bow. Well, many have tried to lift it, but all have failed. Tomorrow morning we will open the contest with Prince Rama. We are glad you have come!"

Rama smiled shyly. Inwardly he felt greatly amused, but did not understand why. King Janaka read his thoughts and felt great love for the boy. Next he gave Sage Vishwamitra and the princes a tour of his kingdom, and showed them to their rooms.

At the auspicious hour before sunset, Rama and Lakshmana ventured out into the gardens to say their twilight prayers. Through the flowering trees they saw some young ladies singing and dancing in a circle around a glowing girl. By mental powers they discerned that the radiant girl was the princess, Sita. Upon seeing the light shining around her, Rama felt a spiritual thrill moving through him.

Just at that moment, Sita looked over, right into Rama's eyes. Not so long ago, they had enjoyed each other as Goddess Lakshmi and Lord Vishnu on their home star of Vaikunta, but in their human bodies they were susceptible to great forgetfulness, so they did not quite recognize each other.

However, Shiva was watching the scene closely, and he gave Rama the thought "you are my wife," and as Rama thought that, Sita heard his thought, and Rama heard Sita hearing his thought! The two were quite surprised and their eyes danced in merriment. They instantly remembered each other from their blue-sparking planet, but they realized that they should engage in play-acting in their human frames, because they had incarnated as Avatars to play out a great drama on Earth. So they looked away shyly, and not even Lakshmana realized what had happened.

The next morning the kingdom was abuzz with a festive atmosphere. Every woman, man, and child came to the court of King Janaka to witness the contest of the bow.

With great difficulty, eight hundred very strong men pulled a wooden cart that held an iron box, decked with flowers. Inside the box, under thick layers of incense dust, lay the grand bow of Shiva. Rama walked up to the box, lifted the lid, and picked up the bow as if it were a jeweled piece of fabric. As he reached to string the bow, it snapped into two pieces!

The sound of the bow breaking shook the Earth and many onlookers fell to the ground. Everyone sat motionless, in awe of that being named Rama. Many felt elevated to high states of consciousness. Others felt woozy and overwhelmed by it all. Each person experienced the event according to the level of their spiritual awareness.

King Janaka clapped his hands in glee, and began planning the wedding arrangements with the high priests. It was decided that Rama would marry Sita, Lakshmana would marry Sita's sister Urmila, and Bharata and Shatrughna would marry

King Janaka's nieces Mandavi and Shrutakirti. Word was sent immediately to Ayodhya that King Dasaratha should begin the journey to Mithila.

Rama and Sita smiled at each other, and secretly communicated their joys through mental messages. Then, at the auspicious moment, Sita placed the jai-mala, the flower garland of victory, around Rama's neck. As he inhaled the heady scent of the jasmine flowers, he felt quite lovesick. Sita absorbed Rama's energies, and they exchanged secret mental love thoughts that even the wise sages could not read.

Within a few days, the kingdom was decked out for the wedding festivities. King Dasaratha arrived with his Queens, along with Bharata, Shatrughna, and every man, woman, and child who was able to make the journey from Ayodhya. The dusty caravan was alive with joy and merriment of many kinds. Musicians and entertainers danced about the carts filled with colorful fabrics, spices, and jewels.

As they approached, Rama enjoyed the aroma wafting from the kitchen wagons, which carried the familiar foods of his childhood. In that moment he realized that he was transforming from child to man. Soon he would be married and one day he would have children of his own. He felt nostalgic for the past, but also excited for the future.

The sound of brass trumpets resounded through all the quarters as King Dasaratha's clan happily entered Mithila. Both families felt thrilled about the engagements. That evening many gifts were given, delicious foods were shared, and everyone sang and danced all around the kingdom. Then they all retired into happy, happy sleep.

The next day the wedding ceremonies began, and as the priests sang the sacred mantras, with incense burning, the radiant young couples walked around the holy fire. The Fire God, Agni, appeared to witness the marriages.

In the skies above, Shiva, Kakabhushundi (the sage- crow who narrates the Ramayana), and many other gods, goddesses, saints, and celestial beings appeared in various discs and other spacecrafts, in which they hovered to witness the happy weddings. When the high priest pronounced them all officially married, the celestial beings showered down perfumed petals made of light, while beating on copper-drums and singing songs of felicity that vibrated out through all the spheres. The Queen Mothers waved sacred lamps which blessed all the beings in all the dimensions.

After many days of blissful wedding celebrations, Sage Vishwamitra announced that his work in the story was done, and he would be departing immediately for the Himalayan mountains. As that man of fire walked away from Mithila, with his brown skin shimmering with coppery stardust, everyone stood transfixed, watching him go. As his radiant form grew smaller and smaller in the distance, Rama inwardly thanked his brilliant teacher Vishwamitra.

The next morning, King Janaka gave his blessings and bid farewell to the Ayodhya-bound caravan, consisting of King Dasaratha, his Queens, his sons and their new wives, and everyone else who had made the jovial journey.

The wedding celebrations continued as they traveled, and so they almost did not notice this spectacle along the way: Parashurama, an axe-bearing incarnation of Vishnu, stood with his mouth wide open, staring at Rama.

In past versions of the Ramayana, there was a big dramatic confrontation between the two aspects of Vishnu, but this time, the wild one was instantly elevated by the Radiant Light of Rama, and he simply surrendered his axe, renounced violence forever, and headed for the holy Himalayan mountains to sit in silent meditation through the ages. (Parashurama had attempted to rid the Earth of evil using the mode of violence, which does not ever work.)

Rama merely smiled at that other Avatar, and continued to enjoy the wedding party. Glancing at Sita, he thought that life can really be as dramatic or as calm as we choose for it to be. Sita heard his thought and silently agreed. Together, they entered the City of Ayodhya in a state of serene peace.

Thus began twelve happy years in King Dasaratha's palaces.

This ends Book One of Vegan Ramayana.
May all be blessed by every word of this sacred story.
Om Namah Shivaya.

Book Two

Griefs Felt in Human Bodies

The twelve happy years in Ayodhya flew by quickly, with joy in every quarter. Everyone in the kingdom felt that there was something very special about Rama and his wife Sita. The four royal brothers loved each other deeply, and they enjoyed many cheerful days in the gardens with their wives. With innocent hearts, none were aware that this was the calm before the storm.

One rainy afternoon Queen Kaikeyi's brother arrived at the palace, and requested that her son Bharata go with him to visit his maternal grandparents in a distant kingdom. King Dasaratha gave his blessings for Bharata and Shatrughna to make the journey with their uncle.

The next morning, when King Dasaratha looked in the mirror, he was shocked to suddenly see that he had grown old! He mused that age can really sneak up on a person. With that thought came a whole cluster of anxious thoughts. His mind began to run in all directions like a band of wild horses. Reigning in the thoughts, he firmly decided that he should immediately crown Rama as Yuvaraja, making him officially the heir to the throne.

The King rushed early to the court, and sat in meditation until his advisors, priests, and ministers arrived. After the opening prayers, he announced his decision to crown Rama the very next morning. His guru, Vasishtha, inwardly questioned the haste of that decision, but outwardly he nodded in agreement and began the preparations.

Rama was called to the court and given instructions for the spiritual practices he should do that evening. He readily agreed, in accordance with his easy-going nature.

Word spread quickly through the kingdom, and everyone became very busy: cleaning the streets and sprinkling them with sandalwood scented waters, hanging colorful banners and flags, stringing flower garlands, cooking specially spiced cuisines, playing musical instruments, singing joyful songs, lighting lamps and incense, and laying out their adornments for the next day's events.

Queen Kaikeyi's servant, a hunch-backed woman named Manthara, noticed the festive atmosphere, and asked what was going on. Someone excitedly told her that Rama was going to be crowned as the heir to the throne. Upon hearing what was glad tidings for everyone else, that crooked woman felt a shock of ill-will shoot through her veins. She rushed immediately to her Queen's chamber, where she found the beautiful Kaikeyi sorting through her jewels.

"What are you doing?" hissed Manthara.

"I'm picking out my adornments for Rama's installation to the throne," Kaikeyi said innocently.

"Stupid woman! Can't you see what is happening? As soon as your son left the kingdom, your husband suddenly decided to crown Rama as Yuvaraja. Once that happens, his mother Kausalya will make you her slave, and you will no longer be the King's favorite wife."

Kaikeyi laughed at that absurdity. "Silly Manthara, I will always be his favorite wife. And I love Rama as dearly as my own son, so I am happy to see him crowned. This is a time for celebration. Here, take this gift from me, this auspicious mala made of rubies."

Manthara threw the precious jewels on the floor, and continued her tirade. "Kaikeyi, I have served you since you were a child, and you have always listened to my wisdom. Hear me now: Kausalya is extremely jealous of you and she will use this event to harm your relationship with your husband. Mark my words."

As Manthara was speaking, Kaikeyi's mind began clouding with anxiety. Gradually fear took over her sweet loving heart. She forgot her love for Rama, and became consumed by her own fears. With her body shaking and her eyes flashing fire, she asked her servant what she should do.

Manthara was quick to give advice: "Go to the chamber of anger and when the King finds you there, remind him of the two boons he granted you long ago when you saved his life during a war. After he promises to fulfill those wishes, ask that Rama be banished to the forest for fourteen years, and your son Bharata be crowned as Yuvaraja. Hurry, the sun is setting. Go at once to the sulking room."

As Kaikeyi walked nervously to the chamber of angry protest, she could hear festive sounds in all directions. The kingdom was alive with radiant joy as she entered the depths of her own darkness. She threw herself on the floor and began sobbing and moaning like a crazy woman.

After the twilight prayers King Dasaratha rushed to his favorite wife's apartments. He felt extremely happy, but he also felt very tired from the busy day, so he was very much looking forward to a relaxing evening with Kaikeyi.

As he entered her chamber, he enjoyed the pleasing aroma of Manthara's skillful cooking and the thrilling fragrance of the incense burning in large bronze pots. He sighed with great relief that soon he would be in the loving arms of his sweet wife. He sat on her golden couch, feeling old but content with life.

After some time passed, the King began to feel impatient. He rang a brass bell, and Manthara appeared with a crooked smile. She informed him that Kaikeyi had gone to the sulking room.

With growing irritation, he made his way to the chamber of anger, where he found his lovely wife writhing on the floor amidst her torn sari and scarves. In the darkness of the room, the King saw all of her jewels sparkling on the floor like the stars glittering on the ocean waves at night.

"My dear one! What is the meaning of this mood? Haven't you heard the joyous news? Our beloved son Rama will be crowned Yuvaraja tomorrow morning!"

Kaikeyi looked up at him, with tears streaming from eyes red with anger. In a voice not her own she replied, "You mean Kausalya's son Rama!" Sobbing, she banged her head on the floor and beat her breasts. The bewildered King started to speak, but just then she raised her wild head like an angry cobra, and demanded that he promise to fulfill the two boons he had granted her long ago.

"Yes, of course, darling, I'll give you anything you ask for. But please, give up this dark mood and adorn yourself so we can enjoy this stellar night together."

Kaikeyi ignored his gentle tone and rose up even more fierce, like a wave rising in a tsunami. She stood and invoked all the gods and goddesses and elements to be her witnesses that the King had just given his word that he would grant her the two wishes. At that, the King began to feel nervous.

In the next breath, she demanded that he banish Rama to the forest for fourteen years and install her son Bharata as Yuvaraja.

The King swooned, and cried out in panic, "No! Not our dear Rama! How could you say such a thing? Did someone put poison in your drink? Surely you do not really want to send Rama away. We can install Bharata as Yuvaraja if you really insist, but please let Rama stay in the kingdom!"

Kaikeyi saw weakness in her husband's plea, which only strengthened her rage. With utter resolution she decreed: "Absolutely not. Rama must be exiled to the forest at once. You promised to grant my two wishes. If you do not keep your word, that will be a stain forever on the glory of the righteous Solar Dynasty. A King must keep his word!"

The King felt a sharp pain in his chest and fell to the floor unconscious. When he came to, it was the middle of the night, and his vision was blurred, but he could see a radiant figure entering the room. His snake of a wife had summoned Rama to his father's presence.

Rama touched his father's feet and asked him what all the gloom was about. The King was unable to speak through his choking sobs, so Mother Kaikeyi explained everything that had transpired. Rama took one deep breath, which he used to transmute the shock into steadiness, and then he spoke in his ever calm voice, "Very well, Mother, I will depart for the forest this very day."

As Rama left the room, he heard his father's sobs growing louder, but he kept walking without looking back. He entered Queen Kausalya's apartments, where he found his mother sitting at her altar praying to Maha~Vishnu to protect Rama as Yuvaraja. She turned to her son and welcomed him with a glad heart, assuming he was coming to receive her early morning blessings for his coronation.

Rama's face looked as cheerful as ever when he told her the shocking news about his exile. Kausalya broke down weeping and nearly fainted. Just then Lakshmana entered the room, full of spit and fire. He had just heard the dreadful news, and with burning eyes he was threatening to kill Mother Kaikeyi.

At that moment, Lakshmana's mother Sumitra arrived with her usual aura of grace. She calmed her son, and offered loving support to Kausalya. They embraced each other in tears.

Something about all that human drama made Rama feel very calm inside. In that moment, he did not need Shiva to remind him of his divinity. He clearly remembered that he was an Avatar of the very Maha~Vishnu whom his mother was praying to, and he smiled inwardly at the irony of the situation.

All of the Ramayanas throughout the spheres flashed through his awareness, and he understood that Goddess Saraswati had acted through Manthara and Kaikeyi, because he needed to be exiled to the forest for the story to move along. He explained all of this to his mothers and brother, which completely calmed them all down.

Lakshmana then insisted that he would accompany Rama to the forest, and Mother Kausalya gave them her blessings. The two brothers touched her feet, then they received the blessings of Mother Sumitra and touched her feet. Without hesitation they discarded their royal clothes and adornments and put on the plain bark garments that are worn by forest sages. Gathering some baskets and spades, they rushed to Sita, who was already dressed in the brown fabric made of tree bark. Rama laughed, and with his merry eyes twinkling, he teased his wife: "So you think you're going to the forest with us, eh?"

Sita laughed with him, saying, "You know I'm going. I always go with you to the forest, in every Ramayana!" Lakshmana laughed along, and they hurried to say farewell to the King and Mother Kaikeyi.

The sun was just rising and the people in the kingdom were waking with joyful hearts. But inside the palace, the darkness was deepening. Rama, Sita, and Lakshmana found the King passed out on the floor, with Mother Kaikeyi giving orders to Guru Vasishtha to tell the court about the changes in the program. What a strange turning of events!

The forest-bound trio touched the feet of their father and guru, and silently turned to leave. Just then, the shrill voice of Mother Kaikeyi stopped them in their tracks. "Wait! It is not proper for Sita to go to the forest dressed in tree bark. She should go dressed in red and gold fabrics and adorned with all of her jewels!"

Sita looked at Rama, and he nodded approval, so they waited for the princess to change into royal finery. As they left the palace, they could hear the King wailing, and Sita asked Rama, "Why didn't you explain to your father and Mother Kaikeyi the deeper reasons for our exile?" Rama explained that their minds were not yet ready to expand, so they would not have believed the truth of the story.

When the people of the kingdom saw Rama, Sita, and Lakshmana walking barefoot away from the palace, they realized that something had gone awry with the plans, so they rushed to gather around the trio. Everyone was pushing and asking a thousand questions, and Rama sensed that they needed to just get out of there quickly, so he mentally summoned Sumantra, the charioteer, who appeared immediately and drove them quickly out of the palace gates. The people cried and blamed the fates for taking their Rama away.

King Dasaratha ran out to the gates yelling after them, so Rama told Sumantra to drive faster. Soon they were out of the King's sight, and he fell to the dust bemoaning his fate. The Queens helped him back into the palace, where he fell onto a couch with Kausalya and Sumitra attending to him.

The King had banished Kaikeyi from his sight before going out to the gates, declaring that she was no longer his wife. Now she sat alone, feeling triumphant that her son would soon be crowned as Yuvaraja. She did not feel any compassion for her husband's grief-stricken state. Upon hearing his anguished moans, she felt disgusted by his weakness, and her heart hardened even more.

Meanwhile, Sita was asking Rama, "Isn't there something you could do to help your father? Perhaps you could invoke the elevating mantras that Sage Vishwamitra taught you? Couldn't those mantras elevate your father like they elevated Tataka and Subahu?"

Rama smiled at his wise wife. She always asked the right questions. "Yes," he said, "First I will mentally communicate with Mother Kausalya and Mother Sumitra, who are sitting with him now." As the chariot sped towards the river, Rama closed his eyes and sent mental messages to the Mothers, letting them know that he was going to invoke the elevating mantras to open his father's mind. They heard his thoughts and closed their eyes in meditation.

A few minutes later, the King suddenly opened his eyes wide and exclaimed, "I can see again! This is a miracle! And I have just seen a grand vision of all the Ramayanas!" He stood up and announced, "My beautiful wives, adorn each other, and anoint yourselves with sandalwood paste, and then let us be off on a picnic in the gardens!"

The Queens were delighted and hurried about preparing for the outing. The King took his bath and they headed out toward the gardens. On the way, they saw all the people of the kingdom lying down everywhere, crying in the dust. The King whispered to the Queens, "Later on these people will come to understand why Rama had to depart for the forest exile." The Queens smiled at each other, amazed at the magic that Rama had just worked.

The three spread a blanket and sat down to enjoy the flowers and trees and birds. Closing their eyes, they entered deep states of meditation. While they were thus absorbed, they did not hear the commotion at the edge of the city. All of those weeping people had picked themselves up and determined to follow Rama into the forest!

Later that day, as Sumantra stopped the chariot at the banks of the River Tamasa, Rama heard the people approaching, so he devised a plan to trick them into heading back into the city.

The next day Sumantra drove the trio to the banks of the holy River Ganga. After taking their baths and worshipping the setting sun, Rama gently explained that it was time for the charioteer to return to Ayodhya. Sumantra was a kind-hearted man, wizened and weathered by the years, and he understood the deeper workings of destiny, but still it broke his heart to leave the young ones behind.

Rama and Lakshmana matted their hair with some sap of the sacred banyan tree, and coiled it up in top-knots such as the forest rishis wear. Next they met their old friend Guha, who was the king of a forest tribe, and a boatman as well. They asked him to ferry them across the Ganga, and he agreed to take them the next morning.

That evening they enjoyed a meal of savory roots, mushrooms, and greens, around a sacred fire. Guha explained that in past Ramayanas he had been called Guha the Hunter, but this time Shiva had informed him that he would be known as Guha the Gatherer. He chuckled as he shared that he had always worshipped the holy trees as God, and now it just made sense for him to lay down his bow and arrows and stop killing animals for food. Also he was no longer wearing animal hides and bones. Now he wore plant materials, similar to the bark garments of the rishis. Rama smiled to hear those elevated tales.

Under a star-filled sky, they ate sweet forest berries and sang merry songs. Rama, Sita, and Lakshmana very much enjoyed the evening with Guha's tribe, and that night they slept well under the trees.

In the morning, after taking their baths and performing their worship of the rising sun, Guha rowed them across the River Ganga in a colorful boat decked with bells and flowers. Sita prayed to the Spirit of the River, the Goddess Ganga Ma, for the trio to be protected during their forest exile.

Upon reaching the other side, Sita offered a golden ring to Guha, but he declined, saying that they were like family to him. With tear-filled eyes, he touched their feet and bid them farewell. Rama embraced him and assured him that they would meet again in fourteen years.

The three exiles walked all day, delighting in every green leaf and every little songbird. The beauty of the woods made their spirits soar. That night they slept under a holy banyan tree, and the next day they arrived at the hermitage of the great Sage Bharadwaja. He served them a nourishing meal of roots and nuts, and showed them a mental map of the surrounding areas. By that map they would easily find the sacred mountain, Chitrakuta, where they could live in peace.

The next day they continued on their journey, stopping to visit other forest sages along the way. They arrived at the most auspicious Mandakini River just at twilight. Taking their baths and saying their prayers, they felt refreshed in their bodies and minds.

Next they got to work setting up their new home. Lakshmana magically and speedily built them a beautiful hut. Rama made a fire, and Sita prepared a meal of foods she had gathered throughout the day. They sat around the blazing fire, under the brilliant stars, and felt content.

That night they slept very well, and in the morning they delighted in the exquisite beauty of Chitrakuta. The trees were flowering in every color imaginable. Blackbirds and peacocks were singing to the rising sun. Deer, rabbits, and squirrels were moving about on their morning errands. Dew drops were sparkling on radiant green leaves. The whole world looked fresh and bright and lovable.

Rama, Lakshmana, and Sita spent the morning resting and relaxing. Sita gathered flowers and decorated their hut, transforming it into a sacred temple.

Under the mid-day sun, they walked to a nearby waterfall and enjoyed splashing in the cool sparkling waters. While resting on large warm stones, Rama declared, "My heart was already filled with the love of the forest sages, who uphold the worlds through their sadhana. Now my heart is overflowing with the joy of the natural beauty here."

Next the forest trio found a lovely moss-covered area in which to sit in meditation. Rama became deeply absorbed within the Radiant Supreme Reality that he was, and from that state he tuned in to his father and felt quite delighted by what he saw…

Still seated in meditation in the royal garden, King Dasaratha was also deeply absorbed within the Radiant Supreme Reality that was presently incarnated as his son Rama. The Queens Kausalya and Sumitra sat near him, also absorbed in the Brahman.

They meditated through the day and night, and at dawn the King told the Queens that Lord Shiva had beamed in and shown him the Big Picture of all the Ramayanas, including future scenes of the Elevating Mission to come.

After relaying that vision, the King announced that he had arrived at the sunset of his life; that his end was drawing near. Noticing the concern on their faces, he explained to his worried wives that in every Ramayana he dies a few days after Rama departs for the forest. The difference was that in the past

47

Ramayanas he did not understand why he had to banish Rama, so he had perceived the exile as a tragedy. Thus his heart had broken and he had died of grief. Now he was happy that this time, in this version, he would die in peace.

They then moved to a grove of sacred, ancient trees in the center of the King's favorite garden. Sitting down under the trees, King Dasaratha asked Kausalya and Sumitra to sing Om Namah Shivaya until sunset and then to sing the Name of Rama into the night. And with that final request, he closed his eyes and entered a deeper state of meditation.

Sumantra arrived just as the sun was setting. The Queens explained that the King had entered Samadhi, with his mind centered on Rama. With tears streaming from his eyes, the aged charioteer bent down beside his longtime friend, and whispered in the King's ear, "Rama, Sita, and Lakshmana are very happy in the forest amidst many wise sages. Go in peace, my dear friend. We shall meet again in another realm."

Sumantra returned to his chambers. Kausalya and Sumitra sat chanting the Name of Rama while stargazing. After a few hours they began to see many celestial portals opening in all the quarters, so they knew that their beloved husband would make the transition soon. Feeling peaceful in their minds, they fell asleep singing Rama, Rama, Rama, Rama...

Suddenly, in the middle of the night, with billions of stars watching the scene, a mighty tree fell down and crushed the King. The sound shook the Earth and resounded through the skies. The sleeping Queens awoke quite startled and rushed to find the fallen tree lying across their beloved's chest.

Everyone in the kingdom hurried to the scene, and there was great wailing in every direction. The King's guru, Vasishtha, made his way to the weeping Queens, and then spoke to the crowd in his calm, soothing voice, "Ever powerful is destiny. We must accept the circumstances of our lives with equanimity. Eventually we must all part in death. We grieve for those we loved, but truly, there is no cause for grief here. King Dasaratha lived a good, long, full life, and death by tree is very auspicious. Our King loved these trees, and it was his time to die.

"We shall now remove the tree, which will be cremated along with the King. Sending messengers at once to fetch

Bharata and Shatrughna, we shall place his body in an iron vat of oil to keep it preserved until his sons arrive."

From her royal balcony, Queen Kaikeyi watched the scene, and, feeling ever smug and triumphant, she delighted to hear that her darling son Bharata would be coming home soon.

Meanwhile, far away in her father's kingdom, Bharata felt very uneasy. For days he had been seeing strange omens, and getting chills at odd moments. His dreams were filled with dark and perplexing images. Shatrughna and his cousins kept trying to cheer him, but his mood had continued to darken. Thus none were surprised when the messengers arrived from Ayodhya and announced that the brothers needed to return home urgently.

As they sped towards home, Bharata's ill feelings increased. Driving through the portals of the city, he asked, "Why are the streets so empty? Why isn't there any music playing? Why aren't the houses lit up with lamps?" Shatrughna also felt quite anxious as they entered the palace gates.

The brothers rushed straight to Mother Kaikeyi and felt very bewildered when they saw the evil energies surrounding her. Bharata shouted, "What has happened here? Where is our brother Rama?" His mother replied in a strange tone, "He has gone to the forest with Sita and Lakshmana."

"And where is our father?" asked Shatrughna.

"He has gone to the celestial realms. After Rama departed, his mind was weakened by grief and he died of a broken heart. Well, actually a tree crushed his already broken heart."

Upon hearing his mother's words, Bharata's mind swirled in raging bonfires of grief. He fell to the floor sobbing. After some time, he found his voice and asked, "Mother, why do you seem so happy about this tragedy?"

Mother Kaikeyi answered in a gleeful strain, "Because, you, my darling son, will now be crowned as the King!"

Bharata let that sink in for a moment, and then pulling himself up, he said, "You are an evil woman. You are no longer my mother. I shall go now to the presence of my real mothers." And with that, he and Shatrughna fled to Mother Kausalya and Mother Sumitra.

The young men fell crying on the floor. Their graceful mothers lifted them up, embraced them, and wiped away their tears. Next they led their sons out to the gardens, where they imparted the truth of the story. Mother Sumitra explained, in tender tones, "We are also grieving the loss of your father, and yet, we understand the deeper forces at work. We are playing out our parts in an eternal story. Thankfully Rama awakened your father's mind before he died, so this time he made the transition in peace."

Bharata and Shatrughna looked puzzled. They asked why Kaikeyi had said that their father died of a broken heart. Mother Kausalya answered in a hushed voice, "Mother Kaikeyi is not yet ready to expand her mind, so for now we are play- acting in the usual manner of past Ramayanas. Later on in the story, Rama will elevate her, but for now she remains in darkness."

The brothers understood and agreed to play along. At that moment, they were summoned to the court. Guru Vasishtha announced that it was time to cremate the former King, and then they would crown Bharata as the new King.

As he watched his father's body burn to ashes, under heaps of orange marigolds and stacks of sandalwood incense, in his mind's eye, Bharata saw how he had responded in past Ramayanas, so he stood humbly with palms joined before the Guru, and said, "With all due respect, sir, I will not be crowned as King. It is not proper for the second eldest to be King. Rama is the eldest son and the throne is rightfully his. All of this nonsense created by my evil mother must be corrected. We must leave at once for the forest and bring our Beloved Rama home to be our King!"

When the loud cheering subsided, Sage Vasishtha nodded in agreement. "Very well," he replied, "let us set aside your father's bones, and then leave for the forest!"

The celestial beings in the heavenly realms above showered down petals of light and beat on their copper-drums, and the entire kingdom reverberated with the auspicious sounds of people singing Rama while packing up the wagons.

In a short amount of time, the caravan departed in high spirits. Everyone felt extremely joyful about reuniting with

Rama. As they traveled, the musicians beat drums, blew trumpets, and rang bells. The entertainers danced about, singing songs to Rama.

When they reached the green riverbank, Guha and his tribe welcomed the caravan and invited them to stay for the night. Bharata and Shatrughna embraced their old friend and exchanged news. Guha felt sad to hear of the King's departure from this world, but he felt glad that they were going to bring Rama home.

In the morning, Guha and his men ferried them all across the river, in a fleet of colorful boats hung with clanging bells. Later that day they arrived at Sage Bharadwaja's ashram and enjoyed his hospitality for the night.

The next day, at the happy scene in Chitrakuta, while Sita was gathering flowers for garlands, Lakshmana and Rama heard the loud caravan of their clan approaching. At first Lakshmana worried about Bharata's intentions, but Rama quickly reminded him of Bharata's pure heart.

Sita returned with baskets full of colorful flowers just as Bharata and Shatrughna rushed into the presence of Rama and Lakshmana. The brothers all embraced, and the palace pair told the forest pair the sad news about their father's death.

The royal four completely forgot who they were, and fell down crying together on the ground. The Queen Mothers descended on the scene, and they too fell down weeping with their sons. The sorrow swept through the hearts of all the onlookers and soon everyone began to cry, including all of the birds and animals in the surrounding area.

The low vibrations of that immense sea of grief registered in the awareness of Lord Shiva, and within seconds everyone saw a blinding yellow-orange globe appearing from another dimension. One side of the strange spaceship opened, and Lord Shiva himself hovered in the air above the crowd.

Shiva bowed to Rama, and Rama bowed to Shiva. The two were really the same Supreme Being, fractioned into different aspects. Shiva communicated telepathically with the four princes, and those whose minds were elevated also listened in. The others simply sat in a trance. Each experienced the event according to the state of their mind.

Shiva reminded the brothers that they were Avatars of Vishnu, and as such they were play-acting in a story for the elevation of all beings. He flashed all the Ramayanas across their minds, then boarded his brilliant globe of light, and dissolved into a vortex of space.

Rama winked at his brothers, and turning to Bharata, he asked, "Why have you made the journey to Chitrakuta?" Clearing his throat and holding back his laughter, Bharata said very seriously, "We have come to bring you back to Ayodhya to be our King." Rama replied, "No, Bharata, you will rule the kingdom for fourteen years, and then I will return to rule, after fulfilling our father's promise to Kaikeyi."

At the sound of his mother's name, fresh grief and rage arose within Bharata, and, forgetting the reminder they were just given by Shiva, tears streamed down his cheeks and he muttered unkind words about his "evil" mother.

Rama understood all too well how susceptible the Avatars were to the emotions they felt in the human bodies. He embraced Bharata and said gingerly, "Now it is time for us to tell Mother Kaikeyi and Manthara the truth about this story." As Rama spoke those words, Bharata instantly remembered who they were, and his body and mind became serenely calm.

Guru Vasishtha understood that the royal family needed some time alone, so he led the crowd of people down to the River Mandakini for the twilight prayers.

Rama invited his brothers, Sita, the Queen Mothers, and Manthara to sit around the sacred fire. After singing some ancient holy mantras to honor the departed King, everyone closed their eyes, and Rama used silent elevating mantras to expand the minds of Kaikeyi and Manthara.

When those two women opened their eyes, they stared at Rama in amazement. He noticed that their auras had changed: before the elevation, their energy fields had been filled with dark energies, but now their auras shined with golden light, and their attitudes had softened from triumphant to humbled.

They both fell down crying at Rama's feet, apologizing again and again for their twisted deeds which had forced him into the forest exile and killed his father. Rama raised them up and wiped their tears. The touch of his healing hands soothed their spirits and they listened calmly to Rama's words:

"Little Mother, do not apologize for your actions. Although they seemed evil to the masses, there were deeper forces working through you. Goddess Saraswati spoke through Manthara and contorted your mind so that you would demand my exile to the forest. All of this was part of a grand design that will make sense to everyone later on in the story.

"As for our father's death, yes, it is sad, but it was his time to die. The moment of death is set at the moment of birth, for every living creature, and it does not change by even one second. Let us be glad that he lived a good life, and he died in peace. And, as Sage Vasishtha rightly said, death by tree is very auspicious. Our father has gone to the heavenly light realms. Let us go now to the holy River and say prayers for his spirit."

The next morning the Queen Mothers cried as they once again separated from Rama, Lakshmana, and Sita. Before the caravan departed, Bharata presented a pair of golden sandals and asked Rama to place his feet on them.

After Rama touched the sandals with his feet, Bharata declared, "I shall place these sandals on the throne, and they shall represent Rama. I will carry out all of the orders of the sandals from my hermitage outside the city in the village of Nandigrama. There I shall live the life of a forest sage for the fourteen years: going barefoot, wearing tree bark garments, with my hair matted in a crown, and eating only roots and fruits."

Rama smiled, embraced the pure-hearted Bharata with great love, and said, "Very well, brother, see you in fourteen years."

The caravan departed, and once again Rama, Lakshmana, and Sita sat alone in Chitrakuta. Many animals and birds sensed the high vibrations of love, and gathered around the three humans. Elephants, deer, rabbits, peacocks, crows, squirrels, vultures, and many other creatures sat close and enjoyed the love.

After some time in silence, Rama spoke in a clear decisive tone, "I know we all love Chitrakuta, but it is too close to the city. Tomorrow we will leave this holy place and venture deeper into the forest." They all sighed, knowing it was the only way.

The next morning they began the journey. Like the bright golden orb of the sun entering thick heavy rain clouds, the shining Rama entered the dark forest.

Heading towards Dandakaranya, the forest grew increasingly darker. Thus they felt relieved when they spotted a bright hermitage in the distance. Arriving there just in time for the twilight prayers, they sat with Sage Atri and his wife Anasuya, absorbing the radiant golden glow that surrounded the holy couple.

After the prayers, the sage offered them some delicious forest fruits, and then Anasuya gave many gifts to Sita, including some jeweled ornaments, a magical glittery skin cream, and an auspicious bright yellow scarf. Rama delighted to see his wife thus adorned.

The sage invited them to stay the night in the ashram. They slept very well, with many gentle deer and other creatures lying near them, and they all enjoyed strangely lucid dreams.

This ends Book Two of Vegan Ramayana.
May all minds be elevated by the Radiant Supreme Reality.
Om Namah Shivaya.

Book Three

Dramas in Forest Exile

After the morning prayers, Sage Atri showed Rama the easiest way to the forest of Dandaka. The radiant Anasuya sent them off with her blessings and a basket of fruits, which included bananas, mangos, figs, and a sacred coconut that exuded an unearthly aura.

Under the hot morning sun they walked through some charming wooded areas, and crossed a great river. Then, at midday, they entered the dreaded forest of Dandaka. Dark and foreboding, with fierce wild animals and dangerous thorns, it was a frightening place. Rama cautioned them to be alert and to walk with care. They walked single-file, with Rama in front, Sita in the middle, and Lakshmana behind.

Suddenly a terrifying monster jumped down from a tree and tried to grab Sita. The princes swiftly stopped him. Next Rama strung his bow, but Sita quickly reminded him to invoke the elevating mantras instead. Thus the horrifying demon Viradha was transformed into a shining celestial being who bowed before Rama and then dissolved into a higher dimension.

Sita's eyes opened wide in awe of that magic, and she asked the princes to lay down their bows and arrows. Standing fully aware of her divinity as Sita Ma, Goddess of Compassion, she transmitted her love for all creatures into Rama and Lakshmana, and they placed their bows and arrows on the ground. They acknowledged that in some past Ramayanas they had hunted animals and killed demons in battle, and they vowed to never hunt or kill again.

As they took that vow, Rama noticed golden fire sparks emanating from the bows and arrows. While lying on the sacred Earth Mother, they had transformed into potent instruments to be used in the Elevations. Rama picked up his bow, and he immediately felt its power to be used for the Good of all beings.

They continued on their way, and soon arrived at the peaceful ashram of the Sage Sharabhanga, where many holy men were gathered. They all welcomed Rama as the Radiant Supreme Reality, and asked for his help against the terrifying demons, called rakshasas, who were destroying their fire ceremonies and meditations.

Remembering his vow of non-violence, Rama gave them a vision of the Elevating Mission to come, and the sages then saw the powers emanating from the princes' bows and arrows.

Sage Sharabhanga touched Rama's bow and arrows, and spoke to the gathering: "The sacred Earth has transformed these weapons into elevating devices which will elevate the minds and hearts of many beings. These arrows will transmit high vibration frequencies of pure Shakti. When people or demons are struck by these arrows they will instantly feel the dissolution of all of their vasanas (behavioral tendencies) and all of their samskaras (mental impressions), and they will be filled with the highest love energies in all of their cells. All of their past karmas will be neutralized as well, so the next step they take will be on a clean slate of pure love energy vibrations."

Rama gave his word that they would elevate the whole tribe of rakshasas so that the rishis could live in peace. Everyone touched his feet, and the travelers continued walking deeper into the forest. They stopped at the ashrams of several rishis along the way, including the Sage Sutikshna who chanted the holy Name of Rama day and night without ceasing.

At the hermitage of the great Sage Agastya, they felt as though they had entered the paradise of the heaven called Swarga. Every tree was filled with flower blossoms and delicious fruits. Every bird was fluttering about singing the most glorious melodies. Every creature of the surrounding area was tame and loving.

The sage offered them roots and fruits, and informed them that Lord Shiva had appeared and shown him the Plan for this version. He bowed low before Rama with tears streaming from his eyes, and directed them to journey to the sacred forest area called Panchavati on the banks of the River Godavari.

On the way to Panchavati, they encountered a very large and ancient eagle named Jatayu. From his perch in a holy fig tree, shining with sunlike brilliance, he introduced himself as a brother of the departed King, Dasaratha. The princes bowed before their uncle and he pledged to offer them protection in the forest.

Soon they arrived at the enchanted sylvan region called Panchavati, which was a bright oasis in the midst of the dark

Dandaka forest. They headed straight to the River Godavari, and prayed to the woodland spirits for protection as they took their baths and performed the twilight prayers.

Once again Lakshmana easily prepared a dwelling space, and they set up their new home. At this point, three years of the exile had passed. Now began ten happy years of enjoying the peace and beauty of Panchavati, with its glistening waterfalls, flowering trees, thick green vegetation, abundant fruits, colorful birds, and charming animals.

During that ten-year period, the royal three intensified their daily spiritual practices, and they began to glow with the shining radiance that typically surrounds the bodies of holy forest rishis.

One afternoon, at the thirteen year mark, dark storm clouds gathered above, and Sita suddenly sensed a changing atmosphere about them. Just then an unusual female rakshasi appeared in front of Rama. Dressed in royal finery and adorned with gaudy jewels, she looked hideous with bright red lipstick smeared on her fangs. She announced that she was Surpanakha, the sister of the magnificent demon king, Ravana, and she boldly declared her great love for Rama, saying, "I saw your glow all the way over in Janasthana, so I have come to find out who you are."

Rama introduced himself and his brother as princes of the Raghu clan, and the demoness cackled with glee. She proclaimed that Rama should marry her, but he declined saying that he belonged only to Sita. Then he teased that she should approach his brother instead. Surpanakha did not understand the humor so next she approached Lakshmana only to be rejected again. At that moment Sita walked up, and when the demoness saw her, she became inflamed with jealousy and rage. She reached out to grab the princess and Sita screamed, setting off an instant alarm in Shiva's awareness.

Shiva appeared on the scene just as Rama realized the jesting had gone too far. After all, it was ever dangerous to tease a demon. Rama glanced at Shiva and then strung his bow and shot an elevating arrow straight into Surpanakha's head!

In past Ramayanas, Lakshmana had mutilated her by cutting off her nose and ears, but this time they endeavored to elevate wounded beings, rather than harm or kill wicked beings, and so Rama elevated her with the powerful mantra-infused elevating arrow.

Instantly Surpanakha shined with the radiance of the elevated state. Bowing before Shiva and Rama, she ran to tell the joyous news to her brother Khara, deep inside the rakshasa fort at Janasthana.

Her brothers Khara and Dushana were sitting in their most dreadful forms, surrounded by a harem of grotesque female rakshasis. They were all drinking thick berry wine and telling dark tales. Khara gruffly barked at his sister, "Why are you interrupting us? And why are you glowing with a golden orb around you? What is this silly costume you are wearing?"

Surpanakha tried to tell them about her Elevation by Rama, but they only laughed. Thick dark veils covered their minds, and many wounds enveloped their souls. This was a motley crew that had suffered greatly and they had no ears to hear about spiritual elevations. Dushana teased her, saying, "Oh, tell us more about this Rama! A shining blue being from outer space has elevated your mind, sister? Ha! You have always been the crazy one in our family!"

Khara laughed, but inside he began to feel nervous about this "Rama." Suspicion grew quickly in his twisted mind, and presently he shouted, "This Rama cannot be trusted. Come, Dushana, gather our troops of fourteen thousand, and let us do away with the blue one."

Surpanakha pleaded for them to stop, but they pushed her aside and headed for Panchavati. Rama heard them coming and knew that the time had arrived for the massive elevations to begin. He instructed Lakshmana to protect Sita in a nearby cave, while he stood on top of a hill and single-handedly shot elevating arrows into Khara, Dushana, and their fourteen thousand rakshasas.

The celestial beings in all the realms beat loudly on their copper-drums and showered down perfumed petals of light onto the fourteen thousand glowing orbs, and Shiva appeared to enjoy the mighty spectacle. Rama glanced at Shiva and knew instantly what to do next: he suspended those fourteen thousand in another dimension temporarily so that the story could continue as planned.

Surpanakha did not understand that they were temporarily suspended elsewhere, so she wrongly assumed that Rama had killed her brothers and their troops. The grief demented her mind which un-did the elevation, so she teleported herself immediately to the island of Lanka where she stood weeping in front of her brother, the demon king, Ravana.

With her mind plunged into lower vibrations, the infatuation for Rama rose up again strongly and she felt determined to get that Sita out of the picture. Thus she endeavored to provoke lust in her brother, but she cloaked her words with other motives.

Ravana stood resplendent with all of his crowns shining on all of his ten heads. With his twenty strong arms, he reached out to comfort his sister, then took her on his lap to hear her sad news.

Through many exaggerated sobs, Surpanakha explained that the blue being Rama had shot an arrow into her head, and then he had done away with Khara, Dushana, and the fourteen thousand. She sensed Ravana's rage rising as she continued, "And so I think the only way to hurt him might be to take away his darling wife Sita. She is the most exquisitely beautiful woman in all of the worlds. She is more radiantly gorgeous than all of the thousands in your harem combined."

With his lust properly aroused, Ravana assured his sister that he would get revenge by taking the blue one's wife. Surpanakha smiled and returned to the forest where she hid in Panchavati to spy on Rama. With each passing moment her lustful obsession grew and she could hardly wait until her brother would snatch Sita so that she could marry Rama!

Meanwhile, Ravana's lustful obsession also grew to a frenzied pitch, so he left at once for his magical uncle's hut in the forest. Along the way he tried to cool his passion by immersing himself in cold rivers, but nothing could soothe the burning in his soul for that woman named Sita.

Thus he strode arrogantly into his uncle Maricha's hermitage and rudely interrupted the demon sage's meditation. Maricha had given up the old demon ways years ago when Rama had hurled him into the sea. Thus he had been sitting in meditation in that spot ever since.

Ravana only cared about himself, and so, with total disregard for Maricha's feelings, he ordered his uncle to transform into a golden deer and proceed at once to Panchavati to lure Rama away from Sita.

With keen inner vision, Maricha saw that he only had two choices: to die at the hands of Ravana, or to die at the hands of Rama. Knowing that Rama was an Avatar of the Radiant Supreme Reality, he chose the latter, and transformed himself into a golden deer.

Presently Sita spotted the charming deer while she was out gathering flowers for garlands. Entranced by its beauty, she called out for Rama. The little deer shined with sparkling gems and gleaming bits of gold and silver all over its body. It gave off a magical aura which temporarily made them forget who they were. As the little miracle pranced away from them, Sita begged Rama to go and catch it for her to keep as a playmate around their temple. Ordinarily Sita would not have desired to possess an animal, but she was under its spell.

Lakshmana felt extremely uneasy and warned Rama that the deer was probably a rakshasa trick, but Rama wanted to please his wife, and he was also under its spell, so he went after the magical creature.

The deer danced this way and that way, luring Rama further and further away from home. After some time, the blue prince sensed that his brother was right, that this was an illusion, so he strung his bow and shot an elevating arrow towards the deer.

The deer assumed that it was an arrow of the usual sort, and so he deceptively called out loudly in Rama's voice, "Sita! Lakshmana! Help me!" As he prepared to breathe his last, the elevating arrow struck his head. All the Ramayanas flashed through his mind, and he saw the Elevating Mission to come. He realized that this time he was the one who had been duped. He could have joined Rama's enterprise but instead he played out his usual part of tricking Lakshmana away from Sita so the evil king could steal her. All of those thoughts sped through his mind as he died instantly of fright.

Rama ran over to see that it was Maricha who had died in the disguise of the golden deer. Panic seized the blue prince's mind as he realized the gravity of the situation. That low vibration of fear registered in Shiva's awareness and he appeared in a beam of blue light. Mahadeva, the Great God, reminded Rama that he was an Avatar of Vishnu and assured him that all was going according to plan.

Rama rushed back towards home, and met Lakshmana on the way. Already forgetting who he was, Rama admonished his brother, "Why did you leave Sita alone? I told you to stay with her until I returned." Lakshmana replied, "Sita became very hysterical after we heard you call for help. We did not know that it was Maricha calling out in your voice. The anxiety took over Sita's mind, and she even accused me of trying to take her away from you. She insisted I go to help you, and I could not bear to listen to her any longer, so I drew a circle of protection around her and instructed her to stay within that circle."

Meanwhile, back in their hut, Sita stood in that circle trembling like a plantain tree in a windstorm. Just then a rishi approached the entrance, and greeted her with a seemingly warm presence. Wearing the orange robes of a sannyasi (celibate renunciate), and carrying only a wooden begging bowl, he asked her name and lineage. She replied that she was Sita, daughter of King Janaka and wife of Prince Rama of the Solar Dynasty. Then, shyly following the rules of hospitality, she stepped out of the circle to offer him fruits and holy water.

As soon as she stepped out of the circle, all protection vanished, and the fake sage began transforming into his real ten-headed demon form. He cackled with rage and glee, and passionately grabbed the princess, saying "I am the great Ravana, King of all the worlds, and you shall be my Queen!" Sita resisted and yelled, but he held on tighter, bruising her arm as he shoved her into his magical spacecraft. The vehicle quickly sped into the sky.

As they flew along, Sita called down to the trees, flowers, birds, and animals below, beseeching them to tell Rama what they had witnessed. Next she saw five monkeys on top of a hill, so she quickly tied her jeweled ornaments into a red fabric and dropped the bundle down near them.

Suddenly a great bird appeared in the sky and challenged Ravana to a fight. It was the dear old Jatayu! Sita watched anxiously as the two fought a mighty battle. Somehow the aged bird managed to shatter the space chariot, and it fell to the ground. In a rage, Ravana drew his sword and cut off the radiant bird's majestic wings. The bird fell to the ground bleeding, and Sita rushed to hug him, crying, "Oh, Jatayu," but Ravana quickly grabbed her by the hair and flew off with her by his magic powers.

As he flew like a bird across the sea, Sita watched her homeland growing smaller and smaller behind them. She cried, "Rama, Rama, Rama" as the demon king landed on his green island and deposited her in an Ashoka grove outside the palace. Surrounded by a tribe of fierce rakshasi women, Sita shuddered as she heard Ravana give them the following orders, "Guard her carefully and use every manipulation and temptation to break her to my will."

At that moment Rama and Lakshmana arrived back at their empty home. They rushed this way and that, looking in every corner for Sita. Their anxiety grew as they noticed the orange robe on the ground and saw signs that Sita had stepped out of the circle of protection.

Next, running out into the forest, crying like an ignorant person, Rama called out to every tree, rock, bird, and animal, asking each one if they had seen Sita. None replied and their silence angered Rama. He fell down weeping on the ground.

Lakshmana allowed Rama to vent his rage and grief for some time, and then he placed his hand on his brother's shoulder and spoke words of comfort. Lakshmana's pep talk revived Rama's spirit, and the two set out searching for Sita. Just then Shiva appeared in a golden sphere of light and gave them a quick reminder that they were Avatars of Vishnu.

Along the way Surpanakha accosted them but Lakshmana quickly shot an elevating arrow into her mind and then speedily suspended her in the fifth dimension.

In the next moment they came upon the dying bird, who lay fatally injured on the ground beside the shattered chariot. Rushing to his side, Rama cried, "Oh, Dear Uncle Jatayu! What has happened to your glorious wings?" Jatayu's breathing grew fainter as he whispered the details of his battle with Ravana.

The princes' eyes streamed with tears as they beheld the suffering of that ancient holy being. An eagle by birth, his ancestors were divine beings from one of the highest light realms. Rama's naturally compassionate heart swelled with the highest love, and he reached out to touch Jatayu. The StarFire Radiant Healing Energies of Lord Shiva entered Rama's crown, flowed down through his arms, and radiated from his hands into the great bird. Those energies relieved all of the pain and completely healed the wounds. Jatayu's dark eyes widened at that miracle, and his body grew calm.

Gazing into Rama's eyes, he saw the Radiant Supreme Reality, and breathed his last. It was still his time to die, even though he had been fully healed by the Lord. "Death always comes on time," sighed Lakshmana.

The brothers cremated the holy Jatayu, then took their baths in the Mandakini and said prayers for the departed soul. After their worship, Rama felt peaceful for a short time, but soon he began to cry again, like an ordinary human husband would cry for his stolen wife. Lakshmana consoled him again, saying, "Do not let grief weaken your spirit. Let us take action. Let us go searching throughout the land!"

It is well known, through all the Ramayanas, that Adi Sesha, the thousand-headed serpent on whose coils rests Maha~Vishnu, took human birth as Lakshmana so that he could ever support Rama, the Avatar of Maha~Vishnu. Thus, throughout the story, Lakshmana ever offered encouragement to Rama. And all the while, Shiva watched them carefully, as he watches every creature from within their own hearts.

The princes searched the surrounding area, but could not find Sita. Crestfallen, they sat down to rest on some rocks. After some time, they resumed the search, and in the deep forest they came across a strange looking monster, named Kabandha. With his face in his stomach, he blocked the path and grabbed them with his two huge arms.

The princes immediately shot elevating arrows into the headless demon, and he instantly transformed into his original Gandharva form. Bowing before Rama again and again, that luminous being dissolved into the higher realms to re-join his family of celestial musicians.

They continued the search and soon came upon an aged tribal yogini named Shabari. Dressed in tree bark garments, and shining like a rishi, she sat tending the sacred fire and chanting the Name of Rama. After her teachers had left their bodies and attained to the world of Brahman, she had followed their instructions and sat ever absorbed in meditation, waiting for the day when she would feed berries to Rama and serve his mission.

The princes touched her glowing feet and she offered them seats and fed them choice forest berries. Next she fulfilled the prophecy of serving Rama's enterprise by giving them instructions to go to the immense Pampa Lake where they would find the vanara Sugriva and his four ministers atop the Rishyamuka Mountain. In her ethereal voice, she informed them that the vanaras (divine monkey beings) were great scouts who would help them search out Sita's whereabouts.

Bowing low before Rama, she chanted his name, and became absorbed in the highest bliss. It was now time for the blessed sannyasini to leave her mortal body behind. In past Ramayanas, at that moment she entered the fire and left for the celestial realms, but this time she simply sat in Samadhi and consciously moved her awareness up and out through her crown.

As they walked in the direction of the Lake Pampa, Rama shared with Lakshmana, "I am greatly strengthened in body by those berries and in mind by that saintly woman's bhakti. My spirit soars in the other dimensions with her soul, and yet I am also still in this human body. This time on Earth is endlessly fascinating."

Lakshmana smiled to hear his brother's elevated state.

This ends Book Three of Vegan Ramayana.
May all hearts be full of Rama's Love and feel compassion for the human condition.
Om Namah Shivaya.

Book Four

Elevations of Monkeys

Still in high spirits, Rama and Lakshmana arrived at the breathtaking Lake Pampa. They stood in awe for some time, delighting in the spectacular nature scene: bright blue lotuses blooming on the rippling waters, flowering trees laden with fruits, and birds of many kinds singing under the holy sun. Rama understood the birdsong, and it filled his mind with joy.

After bathing and drinking the sweet water, the princes began to climb Rishyamuka Mountain. With each step they felt inspiring new vibrations. Focusing their awareness on the auspicious mountain energies that were entering them through their bare feet, they did not notice that they were being watched.

Atop the mountain, Sugriva saw them approaching. Worrying that his brother Vali may have sent them, he ordered his minister Hanuman to go down and find out their intentions.

With his deep inner wisdom and his shape-shifting abilities, Hanuman knew just how to appear to each person. Knowing that Rama and Lakshmana appreciated the forest sages, he met them on the path in the disguise of a brahmachari, a celibate monk who controls his senses.

The princes bowed before him, and he introduced himself in Sanskrit, the language of the gods, saying, "Dear radiant ones, you appear on this mountain in human forms, but I sense you have journeyed here from extraterrestrial realms. My name is Hanuman. I am the son of Vayu, the Wind God, and I was raised by my vanara mother Anjana and her husband Kesari. I studied the holy Vedas with Surya, the Sun God, and I serve his vanara son Sugriva as a minister. That same Sugriva sent me down to inquire about your purposes for climbing this mountain. Be pleased to introduce yourselves and your mission."

Rama's smile radiated joy to all the quarters. He instantly felt incredible love for Hanuman. Speaking in his ever gentle voice, Rama stated their lineage and their current mission. Hanuman smiled and slowly shape-shifted into his magical vanara form. The princes looked a bit puzzled, so he quickly transformed into his cosmic form as the Shakti of Shiva's eleventh expansion in his fierce Rudra aspect. In that awesome garb, showing them clearly that he was an Avatar of Shiva, he revealed that he knew who they really were. Seeing the question on their faces, he reminded them once again that they were Avatars of Vishnu.

Next Hanuman changed back into his vanara body and grew to an unusually large size. He then explained that the path became very rough up ahead, so he would carry them up the mountain on his shoulders.

With a royal Avatar on each shoulder, Hanuman felt intense thrills of delight rippling through his body. He completely forgot that he was an Avatar himself, and became utterly absorbed in the joy of serving Rama. Such is the bhakti of Hanuman!

At the peak of the sacred Rishyamuka Mountain, Hanuman introduced the unearthly princes to Sugriva and the other vanara ministers. Many celestial beings watched the scene closely from vehicles made of light that beamed in and out of the earthly sphere.

Sitting around a sacred fire they exchanged stories, which were surprisingly similar. Just as Rama's father had banished him and Ravana had stolen Sita, so too Sugriva's brother Vali had banished him from the vanara kingdom and stolen Sugriva's wife Ruma to be his second wife.

Thus the two exiles, Rama and Sugriva, who both greatly missed their wives, walked together around the sacred fire, hand in hand. They vowed friendship with the fire as their witness.

Next Sugriva asked one of the ministers to bring the red bundle. As Rama received the glittery red fabric of his beloved, tears streamed from his extraordinary eyes. He opened the bundle, and upon seeing Sita's jewels, he fell down weeping on the ground. The vanaras felt quite touched to see such emotion expressed by an earthly prince. After some time Rama's grief reached an anguished pitch, and he continued crying inconsolably until Shiva appeared.

The vanaras stood dazzled by the approaching vehicle, a triangular shaped craft with a grid of multi-colored lights across the top. Shiva beamed out of the spaceship in a blinding reddish-brown light which knocked Sugriva to the ground. Everyone bowed low before the Supreme Being, and he announced the new Plan for the coming scenes: "In past Ramayanas, Rama shot the fatal arrow into Vali's heart so that Sugriva could rule Kishkindha Kingdom. That act was against the last wishes of Vali and Sugriva's father, Rishya, who had declared that they should co-rule the vanara kingdom.

"Due to Vali's anger and Sugriva's fear, a misunderstanding arose which should have been peacefully resolved, but instead, here we have Sugriva hiding out in exile. Rather than killing the wicked Vali, this time you shall elevate the wounded Vali.

"Remembering that you are all divine incarnations of the Blessed Lord Hari, you shall go now to Kishkindha and engage in play-acting for the reconciliation of Sugriva and Vali, the next step towards the Elevation of all beings." Flashing all the new scenes through the minds of Rama and Hanuman, Shiva beamed back into his craft and vanished out of sight.

Utterly awestruck, the vanaras stood close to Rama, awaiting his instructions. For some time they stared at the blue prince without blinking. All around Rama, they saw light shimmering in shadows and geometric patterns like the sacred geometry woven in spider webs and honeycombs.

Finally Rama spoke, "Dear ones, let us enact the play of Shiva. We shall go now to Kishkindha, and in the manner of past Ramayanas, Sugriva will challenge Vali to a fight. I will hide in the trees, and at the right moment I shall release the elevating arrow."

Placing a flower garland around Sugriva's neck, they started down the mountain. In Kishkindha everything went according to plan. Sugriva roared outside the gates, and Vali charged out to fight his brother. They fought for some time, and at the auspicious moment, Rama shot the elevating arrow straight into Vali's head.

Vali's wife Tara ran out crying, assuming he was fatally wounded in the chest, as in past Ramayanas. However, when she reached her husband, she immediately saw the transformation. Vali had always possessed tremendous elemental powers through his daily worship of the Great God Shiva, but, he also had always carried heavy anger issues that clouded his reasoning and lowered his vibration. Instead of working to release his anger, he had nurtured it at every turn. Now, in the moment that his brain was

71

struck by the elevating arrow, all of his anger dissolved as he was instantly elevated to the highest love vibrations.

Tara saw the redemption worked by the magic of Rama's arrow, and she bowed low before the prince with her heart filled with gratitude.

Vali felt waves of love emanating from Rama's heart into his own heart, and he invited Sugriva back to co-rule the kingdom. Next he announced that a huge bonfire should be lit in the center of Kishkindha, where a public ceremony would be held at twilight. Turning to Tara, he mentally asked her to bring Ruma out.

Rama smiled to witness the reunion of Sugriva and his wife. Everyone delighted to hear Vali proclaim that from that moment forward they would follow Rama and Sita's example: Vali would only be married to Tara, and Sugriva would only be married to Ruma.

Rama declined to attend the fire ceremony, saying he could not enter a city during his fourteen years of forest exile. Thus, the royal brothers listened from outside the city gates.

Every vanara in the kingdom bathed, adorned themselves with flowers and forest perfumes, and excitedly gathered around the fire. Stacks of sandalwood and cedar incense burned in large brass pots near the royal stage. Vali and Sugriva sat on their amethyst crystal thrones with their beautiful wives seated beside them. Adorned in the violet-colored robes of royalty, the four exuded an enchanting vibration.

After singing the twilight prayers, Vali made a public apology to Sugriva and Ruma. Next the son of Indra crowned the son of Surya, making them Co-Kings of their land. The two sons of Rishya agreed to let go of their past problems and they re-affirmed their brotherly love. The vanaras, in their thousands, witnessed that scene and cheered loudly with merry hearts.

When the cheering subsided, Vali nudged Tara, and she lifted the golden pitcher containing the holy waters from many oceans and rivers. As the high priestess of the kingdom, Queen Tara gently poured the blessed waters over Queen Ruma, purifying her of the times she had been used and abused by Vali.

As the vanaras witnessed that purifying act, all of their anger and lower vibrations dissolved away, and the entire monkey kingdom was instantly elevated. Everyone hugged everyone, and love flowed in every direction. In the skies above, Shiva and many other celestial beings beat their copper-drums, rang millions of tiny tinkling bells, and showered down fragrant red and orange flower petals on all of the vanaras.

Rama and Lakshmana cheered from outside the gates, and Indra released the first drops of the rainy season ahead. Vali called out to Rama, "The rains have begun! After the rains cease, we shall gather our troops and find your Sita!"

Rama agreed, and the human brothers bid farewell to the vanara brothers. The rain grew stronger as they walked towards the cave retreat at Pravarshana, and Rama shared with Lakshmana, "In past Ramayanas we stayed in the cave for the four months of the rainy season. This time we could use our superpowers to travel in the rain, but I think it will be best if we just play along with that usual part of the epic. It will be good to give these human bodies some rest, and also it will be easier for the millions of monkeys and bears to travel and gather forces after the rains end." Lakshmana nodded in agreement, and they took shelter in the cave.

Day and night, it rained, and it rained, and it rained. The darkness and the wetness seeped into Rama's mind, and he began to mope about their cave like an ordinary human steeped in melancholy. Lakshmana ever tried to cheer his brother, with merry songs, adventure stories, and even fire dancing, but to no avail. Rama fell deeper into depression. He missed Sita more with each passing day, and his body burned with the injustice of it all. He could not bear to think about how she must be suffering. Where was his darling wife? Why didn't he hear any messages from her?

One night it rained even harder than usual, and Shiva appeared to Lakshmana in a dream: *Lakshmana and Shiva were standing together at the edge of a high stone cliff. Adorned with thousands of snakes, and with his long wild coppery locks blowing in the wind, Shiva whispered in Lakshmana's ear, "Remember that you are Adi Sesha, the thousand-headed serpent on whom Maha~Vishnu rests out in the cosmic ocean of coconut milk.*

73

Continue your good work imparting enthusiasm to Rama. Always remember that he is the Primordial Being who you support. Hold his depression on your head, and know that when it shifts into rage, I will appear."

Over the next few days the rains lessened, and when the holy sun appeared Rama felt a glimmer of hope stirring in his heart. His mind cleared, and he asked his brother, "Where are Vali and Sugriva and the millions of monkeys and bears? They promised to search for Sita as soon as the rains ended."

The brothers sat in meditation, and through mental powers they tuned in to Kishkindha Kingdom and saw the cause of the delay: the vanaras had completely forgotten the elevated state, and for the entire rainy season they had been indulging in the pleasures of the senses. Drinking much wine and enjoying love sports, they had entirely forgotten about Rama and their promise to assist him and his mission.

For a moment Rama felt depressed, but then, as often happens with human beings, the depression quickly shifted into rage. That low vibration of anger registered immediately in Shiva's awareness, and as promised in Lakshmana's dream, he appeared instantly.

Speaking in his ever soothing voice of dispassion, Shiva instructed the brothers, "Focus your attention on the Earth beneath your feet. This Bhumi Devi (Earth Mother Goddess) holds everything that happens here in her sphere. Ground your bodies in her energies, and calm your minds. You are Avatars of the Radiant Supreme Reality. These vanaras are ancient, magical tree-folk, belonging to a clan of beings who you sent to Earth to assist with the Elevating Mission. As incarnations of the divine, they possess keen intelligence and superhero powers.

"However, they are in monkey bodies, which are even more susceptible than human bodies to the lower vibrations, negative emotions, and sensual desires. Think of how difficult it is for you Avatars to remember who you are in these human frames. Well, it is even more difficult for the vanaras to remember, so here is the new Plan:

"You may have noticed that the vanaras wear golden crown-like helmets. If you look closely, you will see that these helmets contain sacred geometric shapes and elaborately colored gemstones. Those adornments are not just for aesthetics, but rather the shapes and gems are used as various powers, similar to the powers of the jewels embedded in the hoods of serpents. Thus the vanaras use the potency of their helmets to connect them telepathically with the celestial beings out on their home stars.

"The problem is, they are so susceptible to the lower vibrations of their monkey bodies that they forget to tune in to the powers of their helmets. There is only one vanara who is supercharged with elevation. He is an Avatar of myself, named Hanuman. As a brahmachari, he has complete control over his senses, but he was cursed to forget his strength and powers until later in the story when he will serve the Elevating Mission. Still, he is blessed to never become susceptible to the lower vibrations, negative emotions, and sensual desires, and so I will be able to communicate with him through his helmet. I have already activated the red jewel in the center of his crown and tested it out. He responded, affirming he understands the Plan.

"So, Rama, once all the vanara troops gather, you will activate their helmets so that Hanuman can connect them all in a network of higher vibrations. Then, when a vanara begins to succumb to a lower vibration, an alarm will sound in their helmet, which will remind them who they are, and Hanuman will communicate with them as needed. All of this will register in my crown also, and I will be closely monitoring you two as well."

Rama and Lakshmana bowed before Shiva, and he departed in a ship covered with bells and made of yellow StarFire. The brothers sat dazed, listening to that glitter tinkling, and feeling the warmth of the golden orb rising above.

After some time, Rama announced, "Let us engage in some human play-acting. Pretending that I am still in a rage, you go now to Kishkindha and threaten those monkey brothers. Unfortunately fear will motivate them more than love would. Later we shall give them permanent elevations, but for now play out your usual part."

In past Ramayanas, Lakshmana felt very nervous about his role as he hiked to Kishkindha, but this time he felt quite amused by it all. As he approached the city gates, he assumed an agitated state which radiated out through ten dimensions. The vanaras felt his angry vibes and fled in every direction.

Inside the royal monkey chambers, Hanuman sensed Lakshmana's energies, and quickly tried to rouse Sugriva and Vali from their drunken stupor. Vali laughed crazily and with slurred speech he sent Tara out to calm the prince.

As the radiant Queen Tara walked towards Lakshmana, even though five glasses of wine were pulsing through her blood, her inner vision remained intact and she saw clearly that the prince was play-acting. For his part, Lakshmana briefly fell into a trance as he remembered who she really was.

The being before him was none other than Green Star Tara Ma, who had emerged from the sky ocean of coconut milk eons ago! Seeing the green stars dancing above and around her head, he knew that she was an extraordinary vanara. Exquisitely beautiful, with an electric intelligence, she was the closest in elevation to Hanuman, but she was not a brahmacharini due to her love union with Vali. Her charming superpowers hypnotized Lakshmana. She reminded him of his wise mother, Sumitra, and for a moment he felt homesick, but then quickly he wiped his tears and resumed his play-acting.

Angrily, with eyes flashing red fire, Lakshmana demanded to know why Vali and Sugriva had neglected to fulfill their promise to Rama. Taking a deep cleansing breath, Tara replied in soothing tones, "In these monkey bodies they forgot who they are. Immersed in the pleasures of the senses, they forgot Rama. Please forgive them. And please know that Hanuman did remind them about searching for Sita, and so several days ago they already called for all the vanaras to come from every quarter of this living globe. Soon they will arrive in their millions. Please be patient."

Lakshmana nodded forgiveness as Tara led him to Vali and Sugriva. Instantly the brothers grew sober and bowed low before the prince. Next they took him out to the stage in the center of their kingdom, and publicly proclaimed that they would never again consume alcohol. With mighty voices, the entire tribe of vanaras declared that they would never again use any kind of mind-altering substances. That tribal vow of purity elevated every vanara to the highest love state.

With exalted minds, Vali, Sugriva, and Hanuman followed Lakshmana back to the cave where Rama greeted them with a calm heart. The vanaras bowed in full prostration, begging for his forgiveness. Rama raised them up and embraced them with mercy and love. By inner mental vision he already knew about the vow of purity that had elevated their entire clan. He smiled at Lakshmana, and spoke in a graceful strain: "Shiva has shown us a new Plan for helping you monkeys to remember your divinity. As Hanuman knows, his helmet has already been activated by Shiva, and when your forces of monkeys arrive, I will activate their helmets as well."

Within moments they began to hear a loud clamour from every direction. The sacred sound signature of the cave's atmosphere swelled out to meet the sounds of the approaching monkeys and bears. Rama simply heard the supreme primal syllable Om resonating through all the lokas.

Millions of monkeys, along with Jambavan and his million bears, gathered around the cave in rings of roars and cheers. Chanting the Name of Rama while jingling bells and beating drums, they elevated the worlds with their bhakti.

Rama raised his right hand in blessing, and the loud throng hushed immediately. The silence was deafening. Every monkey and bear stared at the radiant Rama, without blinking. After several moments, he began to speak:

"Welcome, beloved vanaras and rikshas! Thank you for traveling from all the mountains, oceans, forests, and rivers. I bow to the divine within each of you. I now activate all of your helmets so that anytime you feel yourselves forgetting your divinity, alarms in your helmets will sound, and you will be advised by Hanuman as needed.

"With the jewels in your helmets thus supercharged, I now anoint you all to be the Elevating Force behind my Elevating Mission. In a moment your Kings, Vali and Sugriva, will divide you into search parties. You will traverse this iron- glowing globe called Earth, not only to find my wife Sita, but also to enact a massive super-mission of elevations. Be blessed to remember your superpowers!"

Before Vali and Sugriva could address the holy Enterprise, quite suddenly the skies began shaking, and two hundred billion divine birds arrived from many celestial spheres. Singing and fluttering in every direction, the birds sported elevating devices on their wings.

Hanuman's golden-iron mace and the pure gold helmets worn by the Elevating Force were all decorated with flashing lights and gemstones, all gaudy and glittering, such as the tribes of bird beings adore!

So those magical bird tribes had been magnetized from other dimensions, and they flew around and around the heads of the monkeys and bears, lighting up their helmets like a billion suns emitting and transmitting Light. The birds shined their elevating devices onto those helmets which lit them up even more, making the merry animals look like so many fireflies lighting up the forest!

All those different manifestations of Devas, divine beings of light, which were really aspects of Maha~Vishnu, really enjoyed playing in the earthly sphere!

Vali and Sugriva laughed heartily and raised their right hands in blessing. All of the creatures, including the bird billions, became quiet and listened attentively. As per the Plan, the vanara Kings divided the monkeys and bears into search parties, and sent them to the directions of all the quarters.

Before the southern search party departed, Rama spoke in a confident strain to Hanuman, "My beloved servant, please take this golden ring to Sita. I feel sure that you will be the one to find her!" As Hanuman received that sparkling ring, his mind filled with intense happiness. He bowed low before Rama, and departed for the South with a large crew, including Jambavan, King of the Bears, and Angada, Prince of Kishkindha (son of Vali and Tara).

Bounding through forests, with their endless chatter and merry laughter, that southern-bound group traveled in high spirits for several weeks. Searching for Sita in every corner, they also elevated any tribal beings, demons, and other creatures whom they met along the way.

After twenty-eight days, they passed through some very dry land and soon became uncomfortably parched with incredible thirst. Somehow they kept walking ahead, and presently Hanuman spotted some large birds, including cranes, swans, and geese, coming out of a hole in the ground, with water dripping from their wings.

Hoping to quench their thirst, they entered the hole, and descended down a dark tunnel into the depths of the Earth's crust. Hand in hand, led by Hanuman, they arrived in an enchanted underground realm. Flowering fruit trees framed a large waterbody. Sparkling jewels lined the paved paths around the crystal clear waters. Everywhere clusters of gold and silver gleamed by the light of colorful gemstones. Birds sang subterranean songs while fish glided through the velvety lake.

After refreshing themselves with the holy waters and eating the luscious fruits, they made their way to the other side of the lake, where stood a magnificent dome-shaped temple made of copper, bronze, and gold. Inside, the soft wooden floor felt soothing on their scorched bare feet. Inhaling the heady scent of sandalwood incense, they suddenly saw a radiant yogini, glowing like a billion suns, who sat cross-legged in meditation in the center of that temple. Bowing in full prostrations to her, from every direction, the animals created a mandala around the aged sannyasini.

Sensing the joy of their bhakti, she slowly opened her eyes. Speaking in a voice that reminded them of their mothers, she shared that her name was Swayamprabha, which means "the Self-Shining." She then happily led them in chanting the Name of Rama for some time. Her ethereal singing entranced the monkeys, as they beat loudly on copper-drums and clashed their brass bells.

Next Swayamprabha explained that anyone who entered that magical cavern could never leave. Seeing the depressed looks on their faces, she asked them to state their mission. After Hanuman declared the purposes of the Elevating Mission of Rama, the yogini smiled knowingly and agreed to use her superpowers to transport them out of the cave.

Instructing them to close their blessed eyes, that saintly woman worked her magic, and Lo! In the next moment, the southern search party stood marveling at the southern seashore!

As they gazed out at the vast ocean, they became utterly gripped by despair. Angada declared, "After the twilight prayers, let us sit and prepare to die. More than one month has now passed and we have not yet found Sita. We cannot go back to Kishkindha without finding her. Let us leave behind this earthly world of samsara, that is filled with suffering and misery." All of the vanaras and bears agreed, and they took their seats on the sand.

According to Shiva's Plan, those low vibrations of despair registered in their helmets and the alarms were sounding, but in their depressed state they had forgotten what those alarms meant, so they just sat there feeling dazed and distraught.

Hanuman heard the alarms and remembered the storyline, so he mentioned the great and holy bird, Jatayu. He reminded everyone that Jatayu had fought for what was right until the very end. He had not given up the fight for Goodness.

While Hanuman was thus encouraging them, an unexpected thing happened. A bird of incredible size hobbled over to them, from a bejeweled grotto of stone at the edge of the sea. In a raspy voice, the ancient eagle asked what had happened to his brother Jatayu. The vanaras and bears looked at each other in amazement. Angada wondered out loud, "How does this universe arrange everything so perfectly?"

It was quite the synchronicity. Hanuman had spoken of Jatayu, whose brother Sampati just happened to be nearby listening. Astounded by the scene, they all gathered close around that bird being to hear his story: "When Jatayu and I were young birds, we dared to fly close to the sun. In our arrogance we got too close, so I wrapped my wings around Jatayu to protect him. Just then, the sun burned my wings and we two brothers fell to the Earth, landing at distant points.

"Since that time, I have survived here wounded in my cave. The Sage Chandramas taught me how to meditate and experience union with the Atman (the Brahman within each creature), so I spend my days in blissful meditations. That great rishi also imparted hope to my mind by sharing with me the prophecy that at such time as I would serve Rama's mission, I would sprout new wings. Well, I have talked long enough. Be pleased to introduce yourselves and tell me what happened to my dear brother."

Once again the vanaras and bears stared at each other in amazement. Hanuman spoke on their behalf, "Dear Blessed

Sampati, I regret to inform you that your brother Jatayu has gone to the heavenly realms. He died after fighting a mighty battle with the demon king Ravana, as that rakshasa was stealing Rama's wife Sita."

Equal parts joy and sorrow showed on Sampati's aged face. In a voice choked with sobs, he requested that they help him over to the ocean waters so he could offer sesame seeds to the soul of his departed brother. With tears in their eyes, the vanaras and bears sang the twilight prayers with Sampati.

After that worship, Sampati felt at peace, and he allowed himself to feel the joy of serving Rama's mission. Remembering the prophecy, he informed them that as an eagle he possessed keen distant vision, so he could look out beyond the horizon. To the delight of all, when he peered across the ocean, he saw Sita in Lanka!

The vanaras and bears cheered, and happily witnessed the fresh new feathers growing at Sampati's sides. With his majestic new wings, he bid them farewell. Giving them his blessings for their enterprise, he flew north to the holy Himalayas to sit high in a pine tree merged with the Brahman.

After Sampati departed, their spirits fell. Now they knew that Sita was held prisoner on an island hundreds of miles out in the middle of the ocean. Thinking that there would be no way to reach her, they sunk into despair again. The alarms in their helmets sounded, but they just moped aimlessly about the beach.

Jambavan spotted Hanuman sitting quietly on a large rock away from the others. The wise old bear called out, "Hanuman! As a young vanara, you jumped up to eat the sun as if it were a juicy ripe fruit! Then you studied the holy Vedas with the Sun God Himself! You are verily an Avatar of the Supreme Being Shiva, but you have forgotten your great powers due to a curse by the forest rishis. When you were young and mischievous you loved to tease the munis by disrupting their meditations, so they cursed you to forget your strength and powers until they would be needed to serve the Elevating Mission of Sri Rama! That moment of remembrance has arrived, my dear friend. Wake up! Remember who you truly are! You are the one who can jump across this salty sea and find Sita!"

Hanuman smiled to hear that grand reminder from Jambavan. Thus, with his mind supremely activated, he felt supercharged as his body began growing bigger, and bigger, and still bigger. That Superhero grew to be as mighty as a mountain. Roaring in delight, he stepped onto Mahendra and prepared to jump.

This ends Book Four of Vegan Ramayana.
May all spirits be purified and feel the endless possibilities for elevating this life on Earth.
Om Namah Shivaya.

Book Five

Hanuman's Beautiful Lilas

The Mahendra Mountain trembled under the weight of the mighty Hanuman. In some places the Earth's crust ripped and molten metals of iron and copper oozed from the openings. Many wild animals and snakes rushed about, biting at rocks and fearing that time was ending.

The radiant Superhero focused his mind on Rama, and with a final push off the hill, he took the great leap into the fantastic blue above. Many flowering trees joined him on his way. Before his tree friends fell down into the ocean, their bright red flowers touched his golden brown fur, like a benediction.

From the deeps, fishes and aquatic creatures of many kinds rose up to the surface to watch the amazing sight: a monkey flying like a bird! By the power of Rama, anything must be possible!

Hanuman soared ahead, with his tail behind him and his shadow following below like a ship on the sea. Along the way he encountered many trials which he cleverly mastered. Passing the test of Surasa, the mother of sea serpents, and elevating the demoness Simhika, he continued flying easily through the skies.

The Mainaka Mountain rose from the depths to receive Hanuman's blessings, and shortly thereafter he saw the shimmering green island just ahead. Every cell of his body pulsed with gratitude to Rama, and he felt the power of being an Avatar of Shiva.

As he landed on the golden shores lined with groves of the holy coconut, he stood in awe of the sights before him: lush fruits, tropical flowers, and colorful birds glowed in the radiant red sunset surrounding the living green Trikuta Mountain. Atop that mountain the golden city of Lanka shined like a trillion suns.

After bathing in the ocean and singing the twilight prayers, Hanuman ate a mango and then shrunk himself down to the size of a small cat. As the stars glimmered on the sea, the little monkey crept through the portal to the city's southern gate, where he met a fierce rakshasi. This was Lankini, the spirit guardian of Lanka. She swung at the little creature who dared to enter her city, and quite impulsively Hanuman struck back.

Lankini fell to the ground, and proclaimed, "The prophecy is coming true. Ages ago, when Ravana first began dominating the worlds with his evil ways, the sages declared that when a monkey arrives and knocks down Lankini, the end of Ravana's reign will be near. I shall now leave this gate forever. Enter Lanka with my blessings."

The demoness transformed into a shining celestial being. She vanished into another realm, and Hanuman entered the great city of Lanka.

The streets were paved with gold and gems, the mansions were decked with jewels of many kinds, and everywhere tiny bells were tinkling in the sea breeze. Searching the city, Hanuman heard Vedic chanting emanating from a few homes, but in most places he witnessed the rakshasas engaging in gluttonous orgies with wine, women, and cooked animal flesh (primarily the flesh of the human species). Shuddering, he looked away, and soon arrived at the grand royal palace.

Shrinking himself even smaller, to the size of a small mouse, he crept through many rooms until he found the majestic Ravana sleeping on his crystal bed. Hanuman stared for some time, studying the evil energies that surrounded the rakshasa king. The tiny monkey felt sorry for the tyrant, because even though Ravana was a great Vedic scholar and had spent ages worshipping Shiva, he had never learned to embody the essence of the Vedas.

Rather than living the truth of the knowledge he had gained, Ravana had chosen a life of sin. Puffing himself up with grandiose arrogance, he angrily dominated the worlds through power and control. Hanuman shook his head, thinking, "This potent being claims to be holy, but instead he is just haughty."

Looking around the room, he saw the gorgeous Queen Mandodari sleeping on a bed of emeralds, while thousands of female rakshasis, nagas, gandharvas, and many others lay sleeping everywhere on plush carpets, amidst spilled glasses of wine. Some had fallen asleep singing and were still embracing their musical instruments. As a brahmachari, Hanuman quickly looked away, and thought that Sita would surely not be sleeping in that pleasure chamber.

Darting out an open window, the little monkey took a deep cleansing breath and greatly appreciated the scents of sandalwood and cloves wafting through the salty sea air.

Relieved to be away from the heavy toxic energies of Ravana, Hanuman made his way to the king's favorite garden. He crept through flowering trees, fragrant jasmine vines, and water tanks made of precious jewels with lotuses floating on their silky waters.

In the center of the garden stood a grove of ancient Ashoka trees, adorned with many clusters of bright orange-red flowers. Hanuman suddenly felt chills and knew that he was about to meet the Mother of the Worlds. Just then he spotted her.

Sitting on the ground, under her sister trees, with flocks of spice finches all around, the daughter of Janaka wore only a tattered yellow sari. Covered with the dust of many days, looking like a golden honeybee buried under incense ash, she repeated the Name of her beloved Rama without ceasing. Only one adornment remained on her fragile frame: the crest-jewel pin that held back her hair.

From a branch of the tree above, Hanuman glowed with an all-encompassing love for Sita. He contemplated how to approach her without frightening her. As he sat thinking, he heard the gongs of Lanka ringing, announcing the dawn of the new day. Just then he heard Ravana calling out to Sita: "Good morning, my beautiful, beautiful love! Today is the day you will finally give in to me. As my queen, you will rule the worlds! Let us go love sporting down by the seashore!"

Sita continued chanting Rama and kept her eyes fixed on the ground of her Earth mother. Receiving the daily rejection once again, Ravana's charming tone of courting instantly shifted into a threatening tone of rage. Speaking from all ten heads at once, he boomed, "There you sit, still singing to that pathetic little exiled hermit-prince. Look up and see the reality before you. I am Ravana, grandson of Brahma, devotee of Shiva, and ruler of all the worlds. With me you shall have every desire fulfilled. Wake up, Sita, and realize my grand love for you!"

Turning to the rakshasi guards surrounding Sita, he growled, "Intensify your tactics. Tame her as you would a wild elephant. If she does not come to me within two more months, then you shall kill her and serve her for my breakfast!"

The rakshasis tormented Sita with fierce threats until the king stormed out of sight, and then they all headed to their quarters and fell asleep. Sita sat chanting Rama the entire time, although Hanuman could see that she was shaken by the happenings. Ever so softly, the tiny monkey began to speak the Name of Rama, "Rama, Rama, Rama, my beloved Master Rama…"

Sita looked around with searching eyes, but she only saw the tribe of spice finches that surrounded her always. Saying Rama, once again she heard another voice saying Rama. She felt afraid that this was some rakshasa trick, but then the sweet voice began telling the story of her beloved Rama. She fell into a trance listening to all of the wonderful nuances of the tale, which continued right up until that present moment with her sitting under the tree feeling shaken by Ravana's threats.

Next the voice said, "and then the monkey servant dropped down Rama's ring." The golden ring fell on the ground in front of Sita, which startled her awake from the trance. She picked up the ring, and, feeling the vibrations of Rama emitting from the gold, she knew that the voice belonged to a true messenger of Rama.

Hanuman sensed that she trusted him so he slowly descended from the tree. Lying on the ground in full prostration, he touched Sita's feet and felt intense bliss rippling through every layer of his being. Standing before her, as a monkey the size of a parrot, with palms joined he introduced himself and his lineage. Sita delighted to feel high vibrations beaming from the monkey who addressed her as Mother. While joyfully holding Rama's golden ring, she looked deeply into Hanuman's large brown eyes.

Gazing into each other's souls, they remembered who they truly were, and all of the past Ramayanas flashed across their minds. Sita asked, "Why haven't my Protectors come to rescue me yet? And why hasn't Shiva appeared to remind me of my divine status, until now?" Thus she revealed that she knew he was an Avatar of Shiva. Playfully, Sita removed the crest-jewel ornament from her hair and handed it to Hanuman.

"Please give this to Rama and let him know that time is running out. In two months time, I will be served on a golden platter beside spiced potatoes for that vulgar demon's breakfast."

Hanuman received the hairpin with reverence. Bowing his head, he offered to take her to Rama that very day. Sita laughed in amusement, that such a tiny monkey thought he could carry her across the sea. Hanuman understood her thoughts, so he grew to a very large size, and towering above her, he reminded her that he was a Superhero, with infinite divine powers. Of course he could return her to Rama in an instant!

Sita's remembrance deepened when she witnessed Hanuman activating his superpowers. With her own superpowers suddenly awakened, she declined his offer, saying that they had to play out their usual parts in the story. It would only be proper for Rama to rescue her, and anyway, Rama was not just coming to retrieve her, but rather there was a greater mission to be accomplished on the island of Lanka.

Hanuman remembered the storyline, and taking on the role of a mischievous monkey, he declared it was time for him to destroy the gardens. Sita stopped him, saying, "No, Dear Hanuman. This time you are to rise above that monkey nature. As a daughter of the Earth, I cannot allow you to destroy these sacred Ashoka trees who are my divine sisters. All of these holy gardens are filled with living flowers, fruits, and radiant greens. Look around and see the golden auras that surround every living thing. You may not destroy them.

"However, after they set your tail ablaze, you may play along with the part in which you burn down the materialistic mansions and palaces of the city. Burning down the symbols of their materialistic ways will make the rakshasas grieve, which will soften them and prepare them for the Elevations to come. As their buildings burn, by my powers no living creature will be harmed in the Fire of Lanka. Go now, with my blessings, dear son."

Empowered by Sita, who was verily the Shakti of Maha~Lakshmi, Hanuman transformed into the wild, fierce, elemental Rudra aspect of Shiva. With a loud roar that shook the planets, he ripped a pillar out of a building and smashed it on the ground. Hearing the commotion, Ravana's son Indrajit rushed out and bound up Hanuman. Well, it is not really possible, even for a potent sorcerer like Indrajit, to bind Rudra in coils, but

Hanuman allowed himself to be bound because he wanted to be brought before Ravana.

As Indrajit drug him into the court, Hanuman chanted Rama and enjoyed the play. Ravana's ten faces all glared at him while the central head snarled, "And what kind of an animal are you, who dared to break off part of our temple? Where are you from and who sent you to Lanka?"

Hanuman chided, "Your temple? Is that where you go to worship the god of stealing other men's wives? As the messenger of Rama, I, Hanuman, advise you to return Sita to her husband at once. As an Avatar of Maha~Vishnu, he will forgive you and you will be free to live a life of love. Renounce your sinful ways, and restore your soul to the ways of dharma: to the codes of righteousness and proper living. Through the ages you have nurtured your anger and arrogance. Now, by the grace of Rama, you can be redeemed."

An ordinary human being has just one head with one ego, and when it feels challenged and is given advice that it doesn't like, it sometimes reacts in red-hot anger. So for a rakshasa bully who has ten heads, with all of them being attached to defending his evil ways, that sermon from a monkey did not go over very well.

The egos of Ravana's ten heads flared. Inflamed by the words of Hanuman, all of his twenty eyes grew blood-red and copper sparks flashed out of them. In thundering voices that echoed in stereo out of the ten mouths, Ravana ordered his ministers to murder the monkey.

As the grotesque-looking rakshasas rushed towards Hanuman with gleaming swords raised, Ravana's younger brother, Vibhishana, commanded them to stop. They all froze in their tracks, and Vibhishana addressed the tyrant-king, "With all due respect, my dear brother, it is not proper conduct to kill a messenger."

Ravana grunted and reluctantly agreed to punish the monkey instead of killing him. With deliberate calm, he ordered his guards to set Hanuman's tail on fire and drag him through the city. Thus they tied oil-soaked rags around his tail, and lit it on fire.

Hanuman allowed them to parade him through Lanka for some time. While the hordes of demons beat on drums and blew out-of-tune trumpets, Hanuman watched it all with amusement. By Sita Ma's powers, the fire felt cool like soothing sandalwood paste on his tail.

At the auspicious moment, Hanuman broke free and jumped from roof to roof, setting all the glorious buildings on fire. With gold melting in all directions and huge flames leaping everywhere behind him, he flew speedily to the mighty waters and plunged his tail into the salty sea. With the fire thus extinguished, he returned to Sita to say farewell for now.

Mother Sita greeted him with a happy heart, and spoke in her sweet unearthly voice, "Thank you for making the journey to find me, my dear Hanuman. Thank you for comforting and elevating me. Before your visit I was suffering greatly. Ceaselessly chanting to Rama, I endured the many months of this captivity in a state of miserable grief and despair because I had forgotten my divine status. Now I fully remember that I am the Mother Goddess Avatar who allowed herself to be captured as part of the great epic. With that remembrance, all of my superpowers have fully re-awakened."

Raising her right hand in blessing, she sent Hanuman off on his return journey to Rama. The mighty hero increased his size, and with one great push, he leapt out over the sea.

Sita Ma watched him fly out through the blue sky paths, then she turned to her little rust-colored friends. She sang Rama, Rama, Rama, and the bird tribes chirped along. Without her hairpin, her long, black, henna-treated locks now flowed down her back, shining like copper in the sun. A few spice finches dared to perch in her hair. Speaking in their bird tongue, she told them that she was a Woman of Fire, born of the sacred Earth and possessing many powers. Understanding her status, those loving creatures flitted about her in delight.

Many divine serpent beings also felt the powers, and slithering from all directions they gathered around to experience the bliss of Sita's Radiance. At that moment Sita noticed a silver knife lying on the ground. Picking up the sharp blade, she mentally flashed back on past Ramayanas in which she did not know that she was part of the Supreme Being, and so she had actually contemplated hanging herself with her long braid.

Sita mused that if she had found this knife back then, she might have used it to end her miserable life. She thus reflected that human beings get way too caught up in despairs because they do not remember that they are really Brahman. The same Radiant Supreme Reality that shines in the Sun also shines in the hearts of all creatures.

Determining to help elevate all beings, Sita used the knife to swiftly chop off her long hair, with the intention that it would symbolically cut off the despairs which especially gripped the world's females. At the moment when Sita cut her hair short, the vibration of that act radiated out and elevated the minds of many women around the globe, and they too cut their hair short and became absorbed in the Radiant Supreme Reality.

Just then, the rakshasi guards awoke from their slumber, and joined the serpent and bird tribes surrounding Sita. One of the rakshasis, Trijata, had seen the divine truth of Sita in a dream, and she had tried to warn the others, but they would not listen to her prophecy. Now they all clearly felt the golden stars shimmering warm in Sita's belly. Seeing her power, they all bowed down low and begged her forgiveness.

Raising her right hand in blessing, she elevated their minds and bestowed her Grace upon them. They all agreed to play-act with her from then on. She would "play" like a captive, and they would pretend to torture her, but in reality they had taken her into their hearts as their guru, and in the coming days she would transmit to them an awareness of the Atman who ever shined in the lotuses of their hearts.

Later that evening, under a starry sky, a few rakshasis brought Sita a cup of warm spiced coconut milk. As she sipped that high vibration elixir, she thought, "My dear beloved Rama, we will be together again soon," and in that moment, she heard Rama hearing her thought form. Their psychic telepathic communication channel had re-activated! Rama smiled with a joy that lit up the spheres, and he thought, "Yes, my sweet Sita, I will embrace you soon." Receiving that secret love message from the other half of her being, she finished the Shri~Pala drink, and curled up to sleep. For the first time in many moons, she slept soundly all night, with the sweetest of dreams.

Meanwhile, Hanuman had landed on the other shore, amidst the crowd of cheering monkeys and bears. They listened with great glee to the story of his beautiful lilas on the island of Lanka. Next, without delay, they began the journey northwards to Rama. In high spirits, with much merrymaking, they turned cartwheels and swung along forest vines. When they reached Madhuvana, the great honey grove belonging to their Kings, the vanaras hesitated and looked at Hanuman. In past Ramayanas they had destroyed that sacred place whilst drinking all the honey wine, but this time they had taken the vow of purity.

Hanuman thus instructed them: "We shall not play our usual roles in this scene. It is not just because you vowed to never consume alcohol again. It is also because we shall never steal from our bee friends again. Let us make merry celebration here by setting the bees free!"

Cheering loudly, beating on copper-drums, and ringing brass bells, the jolly vanaras and rikshas ran in all directions, freeing all the bee tribes in Madhuvana. The singing and dancing animals carelessly knocked down poor old Dadhimukha, Sugriva and Vali's uncle, who stood guarding his nephews' favorite pleasure garden.

Dadhimukha tried to stop them from disturbing the bees, but they were on a mission and ignored him entirely, so he rushed to Kishkindha and reported the happenings to the Kings. Sugriva and Vali embraced him with joy, knowing that Hanuman must have succeeded in finding Sita, or else why would he behave with such wildness? Locking arms with their bewildered uncle, they ran into the presence of Rama, breathlessly shouting that glad tidings were on the way.

When they informed Rama that Hanuman's troops had freed the bees, the effulgent prince shined like a million blue suns. He nodded in agreement and said sweetly, "Yes, they took right action. The times are changing. The bees are magical ancient beings who create wild honey high in the forest trees. They make the honey for themselves, not for other species.

"Once the Elevations are complete, all the humans and animals will have great respect for these high vibe beings, and so no one shall ever again steal and eat the honey of the bees. Instead, the humans and animals will enjoy the nectar of the holy coconut. Likewise, the forest sages will no longer steal milk from the sacred cows. Instead they shall subsist on the milk of the holy coconut."

As Rama spoke those words, in his mind's eye, he watched the magical scene unfolding with all the bees in the forest: with their magical mental powers, the bees were sending messages through their networks, and then the Queen Bees were transmitting those messages out through the matrix to Sita Ma on Lanka island! Rama could hear them sending waves of gratitude to their Divine Mother, his beloved Sita.

Rama's smile radiated joy through ten dimensions, and just then Hanuman and the ecstatic clan arrived singing Rama, Rama, Rama, while beating drums, blowing trumpets and clashing cymbals. The search parties from all the quarters reunited with whooping shouts of ecstasy. Rama raised his right hand in blessing, and they all quieted down instantly.

Rama invited Hanuman to tell the tales of his beautiful lilas, so the great hero bowed before Rama, and then with palms joined he began to speak. Rama, Lakshmana, Sugriva, Vali, and all of their Forces listened with grateful hearts and glistening eyes.

After Hanuman relayed all the news from Sita, he handed the crest-jewel ornament to Rama. Quickly, the Great God Shiva beamed into Rama's mind and held the shining prince in his state of remembrance, so that the hairpin of his beloved brought only joy to his mind. Secretly Rama sent a message of gratitude to Sita, and he inwardly celebrated as he felt her receiving his message.

With tears flowing from his eyes, Rama embraced Hanuman in great delight.

This ends Book Five of Vegan Ramayana.
May all hearts and minds be blessed by this most sacred Sundara Kandam, this holy Gospel of Beauty and Hope. Jaya Hanuman! Om Namah Shivaya.

Book Six

Elevations of Demons

Rama bowed to the millions of monkeys, bears, birds, and other creatures standing before him. With palms joined, he instructed that Elevating Force:

"Soon we shall begin our march to the seashore where we will find a way to cross to the island of Lanka. This Elevating Mission is not only about rescuing my wife Sita. It is also about us playing out a New Way and creating a New Paradigm on this planet. Our central mission is about elevating the wounded rather than killing the wicked.

"The Divine Light is within each being already, but so many beings suffer from serious wounding which has made their minds very dense. Due to their wounds, they indulge in bad habits as coping mechanisms. None are truly wicked — they have simply forgotten their divine status. The Elevations are needed now. And quickly! There is no time to waste.

"The bird beings already carry elevating devices on their wings. Lakshmana and I will use our elevating arrows along with other powers. In past Ramayanas the vanaras and rikshas were ferocious fighters, but this time they shall be potent elevators. Rather than using the rocks and trees for killing, those natural helpers will be endowed with magical blessings and elevating mantras. Similarly, the maces carried by Hanuman, Vali, and Sugriva shall be used as elevating devices.

"As we march to the seashore, we will be elevating every demon, every tribal being, and every other creature we meet along the way. Most beings yearn for the elevated state, so only a few will resist. But even in the resistant beings, you will see a small part of them that is longing for the light. Even if it is the tiniest shard of hope, you will see it glimmering in the deepest recesses of their minds. Once you start the light beam into those little threads, the beings will desire more elevation, and then your devices will spread that light until it crystallizes in their entire brains.

"Your devices will simultaneously elevate their minds and their bodies. The elevation of the physical body, at the cellular level, is necessary so that the being can experience the full vibration of Love without going mentally crazy and without physically disintegrating.

"Om Namah Shivaya. I bow to the Pure Consciousness and Bliss within each of you. Let us make ready and begin the march!" So saying, the all-bright Rama bowed to the Elevating Force, and the jubilant crowd bounded merrily in the southern direction.

That night they camped under the stars that shone like trillions of tiny elves covered with silver bells. In the morning all of the native woodland animals stood around wide-eyed, staring at the amazing spectacle: millions of monkeys, bears, humans, and birds all bathing together in the holy river, intoning the dawn prayers.

By the faint light of the rising sun, all received the auspicious darshan of Maha~Lakshmi. Appearing seated in a glittering hot pink lotus in the morning mist, she smiled sweetly at the Elevating Force. An owl with deep dark eyes rather too large for its frame sat beside her.

She raised her right hand in blessing, then sparked out into the heavenly spheres. Thus strengthened and inspired by the Universal Shakti, the Force danced into the new day with zeal, singing and playing their drums as they hiked towards the sea.

As per the Plan, they fired up the elevating devices and beamed the radiant light of bliss consciousness into every creature who they met along the route, including serpents, tigers, wild boars, rabbits, deer, vultures, demons, and human beings. Many of those beings joined the Elevating Force, while others remained seated in meditation, absorbed in the Brahman. Still others recognized that it was their time to die, so they peacefully departed for the celestial realms.

Arriving at the southern seashore, the Force stood transfixed, staring out at the vast ocean. Everyone wondered how they could possibly cross the deeps. Rama heard their thoughts and spoke words of encouragement, "In past Ramayanas I prayed for days to Varuna, the Sea God, and when he did not readily appear, I shot fiery arrows into the sea, injuring many aquatic creatures. This time, I shall merely say a short but potent mantra that will invoke Varuna speedily."

So saying, the shining blue hero joined his palms together and spoke the spell. Varuna appeared instantly, adorned with ocean glitter and accompanied by a most intelligent dolphin. Speaking in a voice as old as time, he said lovingly, "Sri Rama, I bow before you and your Forces of Goodness. I hear your request to cross over my waters, and, as in past Ramayanas, I must reply that I cannot change my nature. Just as the elements of Fire, Air, Earth, Water, and Space cannot change their essential nature, so I too cannot suddenly become a small stream for you to skip across. It is my nature to be deep.

"However, as per my usual role, I do understand the importance of your mission. Therefore, I shall allow a bridge to float on my surface. Be blessed to begin construction of your causeway."

Varuna vanished into the waves, and Rama gave orders for building the bridge of stones. Along with the Elevating Force, many other creatures, such as little squirrels and even spiders, helped with the great project. At night some animal-like humanoids appeared to assist from other dimensions. Possessing eyes way too big for their heads, and looking like owls, foxes, and turtles, those space travelers brought some unearthly tree sap for fastening the boulders together.

Meanwhile, in the heart of Lanka, the evil king Ravana stood towering above his ministers. Bejeweled golden armbands shined on each of his twenty arms as he raised them in fury. Adjusting his ten crystal crowns, he growled, "That stubborn Sita rejected me again this morning, and that audacious monkey dared to burn down my pleasure chamber. I am the ruler of all the worlds. I possess the protection of all the gods. How can I suffer any miseries?"

Ravana's younger brother Vibhishana stepped forth, and spoke in the calm voice of one who knows the Vedas, "Dear brother, these miseries are a result of your actions. Even you are not immune to the law of karma. Every action is followed by a result of action. As a great Vedic scholar you know this truth. It is time for you to embody your knowledge and transmute it into wisdom. You should not have stolen another man's wife. It was not a monkey's tail that burned your pleasure chamber. Rather, your own action created that karmic result.

"Sita Ma is verily the Mother of all these worlds that you claim to rule. Her essential fiery nature will never succumb to your false charms. Give her back to Rama. He is an Avatar of the

Maha~Vishnu Blue Force. As such, he is an embodiment of every virtue. Thus, he will forgive you instantly when you return Sita. By his grace and mercy you will be saved from all of your self-created miseries."

Blessed Vibhishana's appeal did not pierce the veils of evil that clouded Ravana's awareness. The demon king rose up, even more fiercely, like a cobra that had just been kicked in the gut. All ten heads grew red with rage, and all ten mouths shouted in unison, "Get OUT! If you love this Rama so much, go to him now."

With great sadness, Vibhishana turned to his four friends, and sent them mental messages that it was time to desert the rakshasa bully king. In the next instant, the five virtuous rakshasas floated out the window and flew across the sea.

Sugriva and Vali spotted the flying demons, and alerted Rama to the approaching danger. As the five beings landed on the shore, Rama turned to Hanuman for advice. The wise monkey hero acknowledged that Vibhishana had saved his life when Ravana had ordered him killed in Lanka. Hanuman also pointed out that positive loving energies surrounded the five, and their hearts shined with purity.

Rama agreed and welcomed them into the Elevating Force, saying, "It is my vow to give protection to anyone who comes to me for sanctuary. Even a great sinner like Ravana could take refuge with me. Be blessed to join the folds of our Elevating Mission." Bowing low before the Supreme Being in human form, the five agreed to help the mission in every possible way.

The next day the Force worked with even greater gusto, and by sunset they had completed construction of the bridge to Lanka! In celebration, Sri Rama made a shrine to Lord Shiva, and that entire massive Force of beings lay down on the sand in full prostration. Then they sang hymns to glorify Shiva, surrounded by the radiant orange sunset glow.

Suddenly a blinding blue beam appeared bearing Shiva himself, and he showered all the beings with red flowers made of starlight. Gazing up at Shiva, with tears in his eyes, Rama spoke in a grateful strain, "This holy spot shall be visited in the future as Rameshwaram, a temple to you, Shiva, the Lord of Rama."

Shiva nodded in agreement, blessed the enterprise, and then dissolved into an outer sphere.

Under auspicious stars, the Force easily crossed over the ocean on the floating rock bridge. Rama rode on Hanuman's shoulders, while Lakshmana rode on Angada's shoulders. Decked in bells and flowers, the merry vanaras and jovial rikshas sang and danced and enjoyed the mirth created by the bird tribes. In high spirits they arrived on the shores of Lanka. Making camps under the trees, they lit fires and rested in exalted states of mind.

After conferring with Lakshmana, Sugriva, Vali, Vibhishana, and Hanuman, Rama sent Angada as a messenger to give Ravana one last chance to voluntarily return Sita. Angada introduced himself as son of the all-powerful Vali, but that did not intimidate the all-arrogant Ravana. His ten heads all smirked and his twenty arms waved the valiant Angada away from his presence.

Returning to Rama, Angada relayed the sad news that Ravana had no ears to hear any sound warnings. The rakshasa king was entirely obsessed with his desire to possess Sita. Thus blinded by passion and lust, reason could not reach him. Rama sighed and spoke to the Force, "For now this is going to look like the usual war to Ravana. His mind is closed, his egos are inflamed, and he is not yet ready to be elevated. So we must be prepared. As in past Ramayanas the rakshasas will attack us. As we elevate them with our devices, we will temporarily suspend them in other realms. Ravana will think they have been killed, so he will continue to play his usual role. His evil vibrations are strong, so each of you must endeavor to keep your own mind elevated."

In the next instant, a troop of one million demons sallied forth from the gates of Lanka. Dressed in black and bearing many advanced weapons, they attempted to attack the Elevating Force, but all of their weapons dissolved upon contact with the light beams emitting from the elevating devices. Light sparks of every color exploded throughout the land, like a fireworks show of grandest proportions. Within minutes the one million were elevated and suspended in another sphere. The Elevating Force cheered the Name of Rama and beat on many drums.

Ravana's powerful son Indrajit heard their cheers and rushed to the fray in a chariot driven by engines made of fire. He attacked with black magic, and before anyone could elevate him, he injured Lakshmana along with one thousand vanaras. Suddenly he became invisible, but they could see flaming blades hovering in the sky above. In the next moment those weapons vanished, and the Force of Goodness turned their attention to their wounded comrades.

As per every Ramayana, Hanuman flew at once to the holy mountains of the north, and brought back the mountain containing the sacred Sanjivani herb. That powerful plant revived Lakshmana and rejuvenated the thousand fallen vanaras.

Rama embraced Hanuman with gratitude, and announced to the Force that it was time to charge their elevating devices with even more potency. Thus, using their superpowers, the monkeys and bears dove down through the burning layers of the Deep Earth, and supercharged their maces, boulders, rocks, and trees with the high vibration energies emitting from the hot ball of iron at the center of the Earth.

Meanwhile the bird tribes used their superpowers to fly up to the Sun. They charged their devices in Surya-Loka, the solar sphere. Surya, the Sun God, transmitted StarFire from the Sun's core into the tiny machines embedded in their wings.

Just as the birds descended and the animals emerged through the hot magma to the Earth's crust, Ravana appeared with an army of twenty million demons. Using their freshly charged rocks, trees, and other devices, the Elevating Force speedily elevated that entire army and suspended them in the seventh dimension. Ravana assumed they had all been killed so he ran shamefully back to his palace.

With deliberate calm, Ravana hid his growing anxiety from his ministers. He ordered them to awaken his giant brother Kumbhakarna, a demon who was living inside the "body" of a gigantic robot. It took great effort to awaken that huge creature, who then grumpily staggered into the royal court.

After the ministers debriefed Kumbhakarna on the recent happenings, he advised Ravana to return Sita to Rama, so they could all live in peace. Surprisingly, Ravana's son Indrajit agreed with his uncle and urged his father to follow the path of dharma. Next Ravana's old uncle Malyavan chimed in, and tried to talk reason with that twisted mind.

Ravana's mind was a mind so wounded that it was veiled with thick layers of mistrust, fear, anger, pride, and lust. Malyavan saw the futility of speaking further, so he quietly left the court, sat down in meditation on the side of a gold-paved street, and left his body for a celestial sphere. As his spirit departed, it sent a chilling breeze that increased the tinkling of all the bells of Lanka.

Rather than deserting his brother, Kumbhakarna rushed out to fight. Quicker than thought, the Force elevated him and suspended him in the ninth dimension. Dangling in that realm, enveloped with wisdom, he saw that it was his time to die, so he dissolved peacefully into an ocean of light.

Next Indrajit, ever the loyal son, determined to conduct a fire sacrifice that he thought would make him more powerful than Rama's Forces. Dressed in flaming red and wearing many jewels, he built a sacred fire in a hidden grove. Saying potent mantras to invoke the tigers that would make him invincible, he stoked the fire and fed his pride. Just as the tigers were about to jump out of the flames, Vibhishana arrived with Lakshmana, who speedily elevated Indrajit and suspended him in an outer dimension. Just like his uncle Kumbhakarna, he became all-wise and saw that it was his time to die. He dissolved into fiery realms in another galaxy.

Meanwhile, inside the palace, Ravana received the news that his brother and son had been destroyed. He paced around and around his inner chambers. For the first time ever, fear gripped his chest. Branching anxieties spread through his ten heads, as his Queen Mandodari pleaded for him to return Sita to her husband. He would not listen. He still insisted that Sita would learn to love him.

Utterly blinded by passion, and thinking that all his troops were already dead, he puffed himself up with arrogance and headed out to what he thought would be his victorious battle with Rama. He still did not know how powerful those space beings really were.

Worshipping Shiva in his mind, dressed in white, and adorned with gold ornaments of many kinds, the haughty Ravana rode out of his palace in a chariot made of pure gold. As he approached the holy Rama, his anger grew stronger, and he reached for the pile of weapons beside him. Impulsively he fired one after the next towards the shining blue being, but to his great surprise, some force stronger than rakshasa magic dissolved each of his weapons as they sped through the air.

With his fear and anger growing in equal measures, Ravana shot off even stronger weapons that were imbued with the potencies of planets, serpents, earthquakes, darkness, and thunder. Sri Rama met each one with an elevating mantra, so they all disintegrated leaving no trace.

In the next moment, Rama mentally worshipped Goddess Durga and then shot ten elevating arrows simultaneously into the ten heads of the tyrant who had tormented the worlds for ages. Ravana merely laughed and the heads grew bigger! The vanaras panicked and ran into the trees, but Rama grew calmer than before. One who embodies the sacred scriptures remains ever calm under any circumstance. Rama could see Ravana's rage rising, and he met that rage with a peaceful mind.

Suddenly, Sage Agastya appeared in Rama's awareness and reminded him to say the prayer to the Sun. As Rama invoked the Blessings of the Sun, the Brahmastra descended from a higher dimension. This was the dynamic weapon used in past Ramayanas. Some accounts describe it as being equal in potency to nuclear weaponry.

Rama accepted the Brahmastra and empowered it with an elevating mantra. Without hesitation, he shot it straight into Ravana's navel, where the demon tightly held the majority of his toxic angry energies. Everyone watched in awe as that "weapon" alchemically transmuted Ravana's rage rising into radiance rising. In keeping with his huge energy, the Elevation was phenomenal. All of his spiritual practices to Shiva bore fruit as Rama elevated him, and he radiated a light equal in brilliance to a billion cosmic starbursts.

Embodying the wisdom of the Vedas, Ravana finally understood how different this Ramayana truly was. This time it was not his physical body that was destroyed, but rather his grandiose ego was shattered. Quite suddenly all of his heads merged into one radiant head, and he saw a vision of the war that had happened over and over in every Ramayana. He saw all the scenes of all the wars.

Looking out upon Rama's waves of blue light emanating over his empire, his darkness was overpowered by the prince's light, and he vowed to lay down his weapons. He proclaimed that this was the end of all wars on planet Earth.

Queen Mandodari saw the radiant beams of blue light flashing in all directions. She rushed out and was elevated by the Light as she reached her husband's side. They gazed into each other's eyes, and she saw his redemption. The Supreme Being forgives and elevates even the greatest of sinners.

Turning to Rama, Ravana saw Everything: he saw all of his misdeeds, his misuse of power, and his abuse of others. Feeling Rama's mercy, he understood that instead of suffering through twenty-eight realms of hell, by Rama's Grace he had been elevated to the Highest State in which all of his bad karmas had been neutralized, and the slate had been wiped clean. He knew that he was now free to live a life of Love. But, like Kumbhakarna and Indrajit, Ravana saw that it was his time to die. Thus he handed the crown to Vibhishana and bid his queen farewell.

As Ravana's spirit departed for other realms, the Light frequency of Rama overcame any remaining darkness in Lanka. It was an absolute laying down of arms. The darkness became light and no longer wanted to fight. The peace spread everywhere and all wars on Earth ceased because of Rama's Light.

Vibhishana lit the funeral pyre and everyone sang prayers for Ravana's soul. Thick incense smoke purified the atmosphere as the crowd turned their attention from the cremation of their past king to the coronation of their next king.

The jubilant citizens of Lanka cheered heartily as Rama poured the sacred waters over Vibhishana and declared him King. Next Queen Mandodari lovingly placed her crown on Vibhishana's wife Surama's head. Taking the vow of sannyasa, Mandodari shaved her head and donned the orange robes of a nun. Vibhishana respectfully anointed her as the high priestess of Lanka.

Joyfully, Rama freed Khara, Dushana, Surpanakha, and the fourteen thousand from their suspension in other realms. They sat peacefully in meditation as forest rishis at Janasthana, with Surpanakha as their high priestess. Next Rama brought back the millions of demons suspended in other dimensions during the "battle" of Lanka. They all acknowledged that it was their time to die, and falling into the ocean they departed for heavenly spheres.

Surrounded by wildly joyful music and singing, Rama gently asked Hanuman to bring Sita into his presence. With a happy mind, the vanara hero sped to the Ashoka grove to give the glad tidings to the Mother of the Worlds. Sitting in the Highest Elevated State, she already knew everything that had happened. She blessed Hanuman and then allowed her rakshasi attendants to prepare her body. They bathed her, anointed her with sandalwood paste, and adorned her with exquisite fabrics and jewels of many kinds.

As Sita walked slowly towards Rama, the radiance of her Shakti knocked many onlookers to the ground. Everyone present was elevated into the Highest State of Bliss, simply by witnessing the glorious reunion of Sita and Rama.

All the gods and goddesses from every celestial sphere arrived above in their various vehicles of light. They showered down flower petals and auspicious perfumes, while beating fervently on their copper-drums. Shiva witnessed the scene and smiled.

Glancing reverently up at Shiva, Rama turned to Sita, and, with palms joined in salutation, he spoke lovingly to his beloved wife: "Om Namah Shivaya, I bow to the Divine Fire shining within you, my love. In past Ramayanas, you now had to undergo a trial by fire to prove your purity, but this time, by mental powers I already know your purity. There is no need for you to prove it. Instead, hand in hand, together, we shall walk around the sacred fire in celebration of our reunion." Taking her right hand in his left hand, the joyful prince led his devoted princess around the fire. All of the witnesses, in bodies of different kinds, cheered and made merry music, whilst sparks from that holy fire radiated out and elevated many beings through fourteen worlds.

Next the Supreme Being, in the body of Sri Rama, turned to address the Elevating Force: "I know that in your elevated states, you also know that Sita is pure. In a moment the Pushpaka Vimana shall arrive to return us to Ayodhya. You are all invited to join us. That magical ship will expand to hold as many beings as would like to ride in it. As we travel north, we shall send out waves of elevations to all the beings around this magnetic globe. Keep remembering that it is the human minds that are dense and need elevating. As per the Upanishads, the mind is the means to happiness."

Just then, a great ocean of blue light waves washed over the sacred fire, and the Pushpaka Vimana landed in the center of the gathering. That ethereal vehicle was a fantastical alive being, made of perfumed flowers of light, shining gold, and abundant crystals. Decked with flashing lights and fluttering flags, it was the most excellent flying machine. Multi-colored horses and fabulous peacocks sported in the flowering gardens of that mind- driven chariot.

Everyone excitedly boarded the magical craft. As they ran all about, exploring its palaces and temples, Pushpaka rose into the sky by Rama's mind command. Next Rama whispered to Sita, "There are endless sacred fires burning inside enchanted caves down below the depths of this ocean beneath us. The wonders of this sparkling blue-green planet simply stagger the mind." With her large black eyes twinkling, Sita agreed, and then she noticed the rock bridge below. Rama smiled hugely as he told her the tale of how all the different creatures had helped to build that bridge. Sita inwardly sent gratitude blessings to all of those helpers.

As Pushpaka approached the other seashore, Rama asked for a brief landing so that he and Sita could worship Shiva at Rameshwaram. They also made stops to pay their respects at the Cave of Swayamprabha, Panchavati, and Chitrakuta. As they flew over the forests, Rama pointed out many spots where he had fallen on the Earth weeping in grief over the separation from her. Sita smiled, and radiant light glowed in a halo around her like a billion golden suns.

As they approached Kishkindha, Sita gave the mind order for them to touch down so they could bring along Tara,

Ruma, and the rest of the vanaras' womenfolk. Everyone danced and sang joyfully to witness those happy reunions.

When the sun began to set, Sri Rama gave the thought that he would like to visit the Sage Bharadwaja's ashram. Pushpaka silently touched down, and that massive Elevating Force descended, singing the twilight prayers. With tears flowing from his eyes, the lustrous muni touched the holy feet of Rama and Sita, and welcomed them to stay there for the night. By the sage's powers, everyone was fed a delicious meal of savory roots and wild fruits. Many tales were told around the sacred fire, while the rishi's students sang Vedic hymns.

At an auspicious time, everyone sat under the stars absorbed in the Brahman. Through that group meditation, many elevations were enacted, through mental powers, in many places throughout the land.

For example, in villages where Hindus and Muslims were battling each other with the use of stampeding elephant armies, the elevating powers first elevated the herds of elephants. The elevators simply shone the light beams into that deep, wise compassion that is naturally inherent to elephants. Once that compassion lit up, the elephants began to weep, which opened their hearts and minds totally to the Radiant Supreme Reality. As the brains of the elephants crystallized into spherical glittering lights, the elevations became complete in them, and they no longer had the ability to stampede with violence.

The high vibrations of the elephants then transmitted into the Hindus and Muslims in the surrounding areas, and they all stood transfixed by the light of compassion entering their beings. At that moment the Supreme Superhero Hanuman appeared in front of each of them simultaneously, waving his magical mace over their heads. With their elevations completed, they felt awed by their awakened inner light and by their feelings of oneness with everyone and everything. The Hindus and Muslims embraced each other, while laughing and crying together, one and all. Such was the Power of the Elevating Mission of Maha~Vishnu, as it was inspired by Lord Shiva and written by Teja Ray.

The next morning the Elevating Force took leave of Sage Bharadwaja, and made one last stop on their journey to

Ayodhya. As Rama and Sita stood reverently beside the holy River Ganga, the billions of bird tribes sang a soul-stirring hymn to the Sun. Sita Ma thanked the River Goddess for protecting their exile. Gratitude rang in all directions.

Then, just as Rama instructed Hanuman to bound ahead and greet Bharata, Guha the Gatherer rushed up to embrace the Lord of the Worlds. Guha's mind rippled with delight in hearing Rama's stories about the elevations of many demons.

Rama explained to Guha and his hearty tribe, "We are on a mission to elevate all of the beings on this planet. We have thus been sending waves of high frequency light into the demons, which includes the external wounded beings like Ravana and the rakshasas, as well as the internal wounded parts of all beings which show up in their negative tendencies and bad habits. The positive love energies of Hanuman and the devices used by the Elevating Force shatter the ego resistance and shrink those outer and inner demons."

As Rama spoke those words, Hanuman was skipping along the path towards the village of Nandigrama. On his way, he met a sinful woman who was beating a cow for not producing any milk. Hanuman touched her brow with his gold-laced iron mace that was filled with amethyst crystals containing high vibration Earth energies. As that elevating device touched her, the high energies entered her mind and transmuted her entire brain to light. She bowed low before the mother cow, apologizing again and again. She vowed to never harm the holy cows again. By mental messages Hanuman explained to her that now her body would be fully nourished by the holy coconut, so she would no longer need to steal milk from cows.

Bowing to Sri Hanuman, with her brain cells all lighting up and crystallizing, she saw everything as Light. She then looked up and saw a flock of wild turkeys soaring overhead. The birds also saw her, and they swooped down and circled around her head in blessing. In that moment she felt the purest, highest love between herself and those turkey beings. A bursting Love for all creatures swelled up in her awareness.

With tears of gratitude in his eyes, Hanuman continued on his way. Speedily he arrived in the presence of the high-minded Bharata. By mental powers they instantly knew everything about each other, and they embraced with the deep love of brotherhood. Sending Shatrughna into the city to announce the arrival of Rama and Sita, they stepped out of Bharata's simple dwelling just in time to see the Pushpaka Vimana landing at Nandigrama.

With their eyes overflowing with tears, Rama and Bharata embraced. As the royal brothers exchanged stories, the citizens of Ayodhya quickly prepared the city, illuminating it once again with blazing banners, colorful flags, and radiant lamps. The streets were cleansed with fragrant waters and incense burned sweetly in every direction. Musicians, entertainers, and jesters paraded gleefully about, singing Sita~Rama. Every woman, man, and child felt the extreme joy of anticipation.

After reuniting with Bharata, Rama spoke to Pushpaka: "Thank you for returning us all here safely. As a sacred treasure ship, you fulfill all wishes. By your grace, may Sita and I now multiply ourselves into billions who traverse this entire planet to elevate all the beings with the fiery essence of our Shakti. May we meet all beings with the mantras and blessings in their local languages, that are appropriate to their religions or other belief systems. May all beings thus be elevated!

"Beloved Pushpaka, after granting this wish, be blessed to enjoy some rest in the holy snow-covered Himalayan mountains. Come to me again when I mentally call for you."

Thus billions of Ramas and Sitas appeared in every location of the globe, illuminating humans, cows, lions, frogs, trees, rocks, birds, flowers, and every other creature on planet Earth. The citizens of Ayodhya became elevated most easily, and they cheered blissfully as Rama and Sita entered the gates of Ayodhya once again. After fourteen years of forest exile, the royal couple, along with Lakshmana, shined resplendently with the inner fire of their daily spiritual practices.

Rama and Sita ascended the steps to the throne of the Solar Dynasty, after touching the feet of their Mothers and receiving their blessings. With their brothers at their sides, with Hanuman at their feet, and with the Elevating Force merrily mingling with the people of holy Ayodhya, their guru, Vasishtha, poured the holy waters over them, and pronounced them King and Queen.

Shiva, the sage-crow Kakabhushundi, all of the gods and goddesses, as well as every celestial being from every heavenly sphere hovered above to witness the coronation of Rama and Sita. All of those high beings showered down flowers and beat on copper-drums, while all the humans, monkeys, and bears below sang Sita~Rama to the accompaniment of brass trumpets and every other kind of musical instrument.

Sita and Rama then raised their right hands in blessing, and all became absorbed in the high vibration silence. Rama handed Sita a necklace made of colorful sparkling jewels. Sita Ma raised up their most devoted servant, Sri Hanuman, and placed the necklace on his holy frame.

Hanuman playfully bit open the jewels, and finding each one lacking Sita and Rama, he threw the necklace to the ground. Next he tore open his chest, revealing to everyone that Rama and Sita sat enshrined inside his heart.

Rama spoke reverently to his humble devotee, "Beloved Hanuman, you shall stay in this earthly sphere for as long as my story is told. Be pleased now to depart for the high pines of the Himalayas. Ever engaging in my bhakti, you will also be present everywhere at all times."

One by one, Rama and Sita thanked and blessed the members of the Elevating Force. With promises to visit often, the vanaras, rikshas, birds, rakshasas, and others returned to their homelands.

Thus began the dynamic, harmonious reign of Sita and Rama. For eleven thousand years they ruled the earthly sphere. Under the glorious Rama~Sita~Rajya, all beings lived in Elevation, Peace, Happiness, and Love.

Sita and Rama ever shined in the bright violet-purple pinecone inside the third eye of all beings, even the squirrels! And that Union of Divine Feminine and Divine Masculine, that Gandhi-ji adored, radiated up the ajna chakra of each being and out through the thousand-petaled crown, the seat of Lord Shiva, whose long matted locks ever shine with coppery radiance.

Jaya Sita Rama! Jaya Shiva Shankara!

This ends Book Six of Vegan Ramayana.
May all minds be increasingly elevated and revere the Forces of Goodness.
Om Namah Shivaya.

Book Seven

Worlds of Golden Light

Once the Elevations reached eight billion humans complete, an alchemical transmutation occurred: the dark Iron Age of sin evolved into the all-bright Golden Age of purity. The reign of Rama and Sita, called Rama~Sita~Rajya, heralded the New Way, also referred to as the New Paradigm.

At the start of the New Normal, Lord Shiva beamed StarFire Radiant Healing Energies into all beings, and that Supreme Healing eradicated all diseases. With no more sicknesses to cause deaths, all the human creatures simply died easily and happily, at the times and places already determined at the moments of their births.

The Earth became part of the Shakahara StarFire Universes. The holy Shakahara StarFire Sun shined inspiring, healing rays that amplified the Elevations and burned away the remaining dross from all past karmas.

Due to everyone being elevated into the Highest State, all lived in peace without any bad karmas haunting them. A Radiant Golden Clean Slate shimmered in the atmosphere. All human beings realized that the Earth itself was alive and as such it was part of the One Love Energy that connected everyone and everything. Thus they began to nurture the Earth in every possible way.

Creatively and innovatively, they harnessed the energy resources available through Sun-power, and utilized new technologies to extract power from other dimensions and galaxies. They planted organic gardens, fruit trees, and fields of sunflowers throughout the lands. Everywhere, in every way, every being rejoiced in the beauty of nature.

All the waters became clean and pure. In every land the people, animals, and birds could drink high vibration water right out of springs in the Earth. Many also enjoyed hydrating with the nectar of holy coconut water.

The air became purified in all directions. Breathing deeply and resting in their union with the Radiant Supreme Reality, every kind of being was elevated to no longer want or need to feed off the flesh and blood of other species. Tigers no longer ate deer. Cats no longer ate mice. Mosquitoes no longer sucked the blood of humans, but instead sucked the juice from plants. All lived together in great harmony, eating plant foods and holy coconuts.

All recognized the sacred spirit of the coconut. Hanuman had transmitted the reverence for the coconut to the Avatars, after asking Rama why some species ate the flesh of other species. Rama had explained to Hanuman that when the planet came into being, certain laws came into being with it, like the anatomy of cats requiring meat for survival. "But now," Rama continued, "the physical anatomy of all species shall be elevated to no longer need or want meat. From now on, the anatomies will evolve to only require plant foods for nourishment."

While sitting in their favorite garden, enjoying the fragrance of the greening herbs and blossoming flowers, Sita and Rama sent a mental message to the eight billion human beings: "When Ravana dominated this earthly sphere, he declared that the human species had been created by God for his rakshasa tribe to eat. Now, under our rule, no species shall eat the flesh of any other species.

"This is the highest Vedic principle of ahimsa, of doing no harm. The diet should be as compassionate as possible. Be blessed to live in freedom, whilst allowing all other creatures to also live in freedom. Every kind of being experiences suffering and seeks happiness. Let us create worlds of happiness for all beings."

Thus, the humans no longer ate the flesh of cows, chickens, pigs, lambs, turkeys, ducks, deer, buffalos, rabbits, snakes, fishes, and others.

All of the animals, reptiles, and birds played and sported together in harmony, no longer needing to eat each other. In the depths of the oceans, all the fishes, whales, sharks, and other aquatic creatures lived in great peace, because all of their anatomies were also transformed to no longer need to eat their fellow creatures. All the living beings of the land, sea, and air now thrived by eating plant foods.

All of the millions and millions of pets around the globe were allowed to once again live in nature, in total freedom, including the dogs, cats, horses, birds, rabbits, snakes, turtles, lizards, mice, rats, fishes, and others. They all celebrated their liberation with a joy that reverberated throughout all time and space.

Each species fed its own young. Humans no longer stole milk from cows and goats, nor eggs from chickens, nor honey from bees. Amongst these liberated species, the holy cows felt the happiest of all. They actually danced for joy, with tears streaming down their faces.

Rabbits, rats, mice, and other creatures ate their own plant foods separate from the fields of plant foods cultivated by the humans. Insects also found other plants, so they no longer fed on the humans' gardens.

Ants, mosquitoes, flies, roaches, and others were content to live in their own natural kingdoms, so they no longer raided the dwellings of humans.

The body of every living being was a temple that was directly connected to all the stars and spheres. Golden auras surrounded all beings, including the crystals, gemstones, and metals of the Earth.

The Elevations changed the destiny of all beings. The Avatars and the Elevating Force had incarnated to alter the course of darkness that was taking over the terrestrial sphere. Evil forces, ruled by Ravana, had created endless strife on the planet by taking advantage of all the deep woundings, misunderstandings, and dark twisted neural networks in the human brains.

Implicit in the Elevations was a total and Supreme Forgiveness of the past sins of all creatures. All karmas were dissolved and the slates were wiped clean. Although past Ramayanas occurred in Treta Yuga, this version happened in the Kali Yuga, the dark iron age, because the human species and the Earth were on the brink of total self-destruction.

In the new Golden Age, under Rama~Sita~Rajya, there was no longer any need to keep cycling through ages with names. From then on, everything just became Worlds of Golden Light. Auspiciousness, Shivam, was enshrined in every heart. Each being knew the truth of "Shivoham" ("I Am God"), because all beings realized that they were forms that had emerged out of the One Love Energy, also called Brahman and the Radiant Supreme Reality.

That Supreme Being pervades everyone and everything in a continuous web of energy. Who can comprehend the magnitude of the Supreme Spirit?

Rama~Sita~Rajya brought all the spheres into the Highest State of Peace. All beings lived in that Shanti, with Shakahara vibrations resounding through every dimension.

On planet Earth, everyone felt intense gratitude that there were no more wars, no more diseases, no more money, no more starvation, no more addictions, and no more suffering of any kind. All human beings spent their time helping in organic gardens, preparing delightful plant foods, singing, celebrating the healing of the Earth, playing with all the non-human creatures like cows and birds and foxes and fishes, creating beauty, making music, adorning each other with colorful flowers and sparkling crystals, dancing barefoot on the Earth, enjoying the fresh air and clean water, and worshipping the Moon, the Sun, the Elements, and the Supreme Love Intelligence of all the universes who had incarnated and saved the Earth and its humans through the massive Elevating Mission.

After ten thousand years of that harmonious state on planet Earth, in past Ramayanas the people of Ayodhya began to gossip, accusing Sita of not being pure because she had lived in another man's kingdom. Rama knew that she was pure, but in order to uphold the reputation of the Solar Dynasty, he chose to follow the dharmic code of ancient kings. Thus he quite abruptly banished Sita to the forest, even though she was with child.

In this Shakahara StarFire version, when Sita became pregnant, all of the still-elevated citizens of Ayodhya celebrated with great joy. Everyone worshipped and honored their Queen even more intensely throughout her pregnancy.

At the auspicious time, Rama and Sita traveled to the forest together for her to give birth amongst the trees, under the stars.

In a sacred stone hollow, sparkling with amethyst crystals growing out of the Earth, the royal twins entered the earthly sphere. Named Lava and Kusha, and loved by all the worlds, those sweet-natured boys played ever happily in the dust. Born and raised in a state of total Elevation, they embodied strength, purity, wisdom, and grace.

When Lava and Kusha had grown to be men, Sita and Rama crowned them to co-rule the Worlds of Golden Light for all of eternity. Shortly after their coronation, the three Grandmothers (Kausalya, Sumitra, and Kaikeyi) peacefully left their bodies for the heavenly spheres.

A short time later, Shiva telepathically communicated with Rama and Sita, informing them that their work as Avatars was nearing completion. Thus preparations were made for the four brothers and Sita to return to Vaikunta. In keeping with some past Ramayanas, it was decided that Sita would go through the Earth, while Rama and his brothers would go through the River.

The radiant Co-Kings, Lava and Kusha, and all of the citizens of Ayodhya created a grand festival in the forest. Humans, vanaras, rikshas, birds, rakshasas, sages, gods, goddesses, and many other beings attended. Rama and Sita smiled to see their old friends, including Hanuman, Sugriva, Ruma, Vali, Tara, Angada, Jambavan, Vibhishana, Surama, and Mandodari.

At the right moment they all joyously witnessed the Earth opening and receiving her daughter once again. Sita descended down through the layers to enjoy some time in the naga realm with her Earth mother and her sisters, the roots of all the Earth's trees. (A bit later she would return to Vaikunta.)

Next, everyone in attendance moved to the green riverbank of the holy Sarayu to witness the four royal brothers diving into the river realm. A few moments later, Rama, Lakshmana, Bharata, and Shatrughna arose from the gleaming waters and merged into Maha~Vishnu's scintillating four-armed cosmic form. As he ascended through the Sky Ocean beaming out towards Vaikunta, everyone present felt incredible gratitude and increased zest for life.

The next morning, under the rising sun, Lava and Kusha sat by the river sipping holy coconut milk. Together they mentally watched a vision of the dazzling reunion of Maha~Vishnu and Maha~Lakshmi on their blue-sparking home planet out in the Shakahara StarFire Universes.

Hanuman saw the same vision from his temple in the high pine trees of the snow-covered Himalayan mountains.

There he sat, ever immersed in Rama~Sita bhakti. Ringing his bells and singing to the beloveds enshrined in his heart, he delighted to see their cosmic reunion, and he swiftly sent gratitude blessings to Lava and Kusha.

Embracing each other with tears flowing from their blessed eyes, the Brother-Kings looked out happily upon the Worlds of Golden Light.

This ends Book Seven of Vegan Ramayana.
May all be blessed with ecstatic joy and deep gratitude. May the Radiant StarFire Consciousness of Lord Shiva Shankara spark out everywhere for the Good of all beings.
Om! May all beings feel the Joy vibrating within them!
May all beings be Elevated to the Highest Love State.
May All Beings Be Happy.

Jaya Sita~Rama, Jaya Jaya Hanuman!

Om Namah Shivaya.

Epilogue

As this Ramayana began, the situation on planet Earth had reached crisis proportions. The waters and air were polluted, the animals were dying off, and the Earth itself was sending off many warning signals in the forms of increased winds, raging fires, and devastating storms. The dark forces were taking over the very atmosphere, and the creatures were beginning to starve on many levels.

In that stark state of affairs, so many sins had been created as a result of the wounded human minds, that if all of those negative karmas had come back in reaction to all of the evil actions already committed, it would have been too much darkness for the earthly sphere to bear. Thus, with the human race teetering on the brink of total self-destruction, the Elevations were required to wipe the karmic slates clean before it was too late.

The great Vedic scholar and saint, Adi Shankara, taught that when a human being is elevated to the state of union with the Brahman, he or she is then freed from the law of karma. (*Shankara's Crest-Jewel of Discrimination (Viveka- Chudamani):* Translated with an Introduction to Shankara's Philosophy, by Swami Prabhavananda and Christopher Isherwood, Vedanta Press, California, 1947.) That is what occurred after the Elevations reached eight billion humans complete. A Radiant Golden Clean Slate shimmered for all human beings, as the high vibration extraterrestrial energies shined the golden fire of Spiritual Radiance into everyone.

Some past Ramayanas, such as the literary masterpiece, *Shri Ramacharitamanasa*, by Sri Tulasidasa, contained a plethora of gorgeous similes and soul-stirring descriptions of the beauty of nature, in lengthy narratives exceeding seven hundred pages. This version was intentionally kept much shorter in order to keep the storyline moving at a faster pace for the busy modern reader.

The benefits of reading this book are many: Elevation to the Highest Love State; Activation of Cosmic Shakahara StarFire Radiant Healing Consciousness; and Awakening of qualities such as Hope, Inspiration, Innovation, Compassion, and Creativity. As these beautiful positive energies arise, quite naturally there occurs a reduction of fear, anger, and sadness. The lotus in the heart opens to the Shakti of the Supreme Being.

The magnitude of that Maha~Vishnu Force blows the mind because simultaneously that Force is existing in Vaikunta, and is manifesting on Earth as Avatars, AND is living in the hearts of all creatures. Who can understand the incredible magnitude of the Holy Blue Force?

In days of old, in earlier times when the Ramayana played out, Rama hid inside the hearts of all human beings, and the humans could only realize that divinity in their hearts by a long slow process of purifying their minds. But in this version, the human minds had become too dense and so the old methods would have been too slow to save the planet. This time the human minds needed to be elevated much more quickly. Thus Lord Shiva planted this question in the mind of Teja Ray: If every human being was suddenly spiritually elevated to the Highest Love Vibrations, what would life on this sacred Earth be like?

In ancient times they foresaw the ruin of this dark iron age, but we do not have to ruin our planet and our human race. With or without a massive intervention by blue beings from outer space, using innovation and elevation we can make life on Earth a happy experience for all creatures. We can increase our brain capacities, and we can remember our full range of mental powers.

Sant (Saint) Keshavadas wrote, "The future religion of the world will be mysticism. Its scriptures will be based upon the teachings and lives of saints of all world religions." (*Saints of India*, published by Temple of Cosmic Religion, 1975.) In every land, the saints ever work for the Good of all beings.

Many people believe that the battle between good and evil will continue for all time. They say that the endless war between the light and the dark is the very nature of the cosmos itself. As elevated human beings, we have the power to stop feeding that negative belief, and to join the saints in working toward a world of Goodness.

Some people may question whether or not these Elevations are possible. Well, we may not have elevating "devices," but we do inherently contain the power to re-wire our brains. We can heal the wounded brain regions that prevent us from remembering our divine heritage.

In past Ramayanas, none could escape the workings of destiny~karma~fate, but in this version, Maha~Vishnu's Avatars, Sita and Rama, used innovative techniques to uplift universal laws for achieving the Elevation of All Beings.

In other Ramayanas, the protectors of the worlds took human birth as Rama, Sita, Lakshmana, and the other incarnations, in order to destroy the tribe of rakshasas, but in this version, they beamed into human forms to *Elevate* the tribe. As Rama explained to the Elevating Force, the mission this time was about elevating the wounded rather than killing the wicked. Thus they endeavored to destroy the egos of the wounded beings, rather than harming their physical bodies.

We are all One Love Energy in many forms. We all resonate with the Stars. Aligning in a Shakahara StarFire Tribe, we could live together in Peace and Joy.

Throughout the ages, Sita symbolized the human soul kidnapped by the demon Ravana who represented the human ego. With the help of Hanuman, the breath, Sita reconnected her soul in prayer to Rama (the Supreme Soul or God) who then freed her from captivity by destroying the demon king.

In this version, Sita symbolized the entire human race which was held captive by the demon Ravana who represented all the sins of the dark age of materialism. Sita (the human race) could not truly be saved by the mode of violence. True Freedom for Sita (the human race) could only come by the Force of Light overpowering the dark demon of materialism and its harmful effects, including greed, competition, domination, and starvation. Ever chanting the Name of Rama, Sita called in the Light.

That Force of Light — call it God, Goddess, Rama, Sita, Shiva, Shakti, Durga, Allah, Yahweh, Mary, Jesus, Truth, Guru, Buddha, Jah, Gaia, Great Spirit, Great Mystery, Brahman, Supreme Being — that Force is Beyond all human conceptions and images of It. That Light is extra-terrestrial, and in this Ramayana, It was most definitely Blue!

Endlessly working to spread the Goodness of that Light Force, Sri Hanuman is still ever-present everywhere. He appears anytime Rama's story is told and anytime the Hanuman Chalisa is sung. Granting strength, positive energy, wisdom, and courage, Hanuman removes fears, diseases, and sorrows. Visualizing him high in the pine trees, ringing his bells, and singing Sita~Rama, brings great happiness to the mind.

This ends the fascinating tale of Vegan Ramayana.
Salutations to that Force of Light embodied in Rama and Sita. May each reader, regardless of his or her religion or belief system, receive a transmission of the Elevated State that is experienced by Ramabhaktas and Shivabhaktas when they are deeply immersed in worshipping the resplendent glory of Hari and Hara.

May the Radiant Supreme Reality heal us all.

May All Beings Be Elevated to the Highest Love State.

Jaya Sita~Rama, Jaya Jaya Hanuman!!!

~ Shri Rama Jaya Rama Jaya Jaya Rama ~

Bolo Rama Sita Hanuman Shiva!

Om Shree Hanumate Namaha.

Om Namah Shivaya.

Glossary

Agni ~ The Vedic Fire God.

Ahimsa ~ The Vedic principle of non-violence. The doctrine of doing no harm, and of cultivating compassion for all beings.

Ajna Chakra ~ The energy center located at the third eye, in the center of the forehead, slightly above the eyebrows. This center is associated with intuition and spiritual wisdom.

Animals ~ In this book's dedication ("For the animals") animals refers to the non-human mammals, along with all the birds, fish, reptiles, and amphibians, all of whom have a central nervous system with a brain and spinal cord. Collectively, they are classed as vertebrates (animals with backbones). They have nerves which are sensitive to pain, and thus they *feel* pain. And, although bees do not have backbones, they are highly intelligent sensitive beings who are included in the dedication.

Ashram ~ A hermitage or spiritual community. The residence of gurus, sages, and their disciples.

Atman ~ The Brahman within the creature. The Radiant Supreme Reality that is shining inside the hearts of all creatures, and witnessing everything. The individual soul. In his work, *Viveka-Chudamani*, the eighth century teacher Adi Shankara explained that the air in a jar is one with the air everywhere. Thus, the Atman, the spirit within the body, is one with the Supreme Spirit, the Brahman, which is within everyone and everything. (*Shankara's Crest-Jewel of Discrimination (Viveka- Chudamani):* Translated with an Introduction to Shankara's Philosophy, by Swami Prabhavananda and Christopher Isherwood, Vedanta Press, California, 1947.)

Avatar ~ An incarnation of the Divine.

Bhakti ~ The path of devotion and love. Devotional worship directed to the Supreme Being, in any or all of his divine forms and aspects.

Bhumi Devi ~ Earth Goddess.

Bolo ~ Sing or chant.

Brahma ~ The creator aspect of the Hindu Trinity. (Maha~Vishnu divides his Supreme Energy into the trinity of Brahma, Vishnu, and Shiva, for the functioning of the universes.) Brahma's consort is Saraswati Devi.

Brahmachari (male), Brahmacharini (female) ~ A spiritual student or disciple who practices self-control, purity, and celibacy.

Brahman ~ The Supreme Being; the Radiant Supreme Reality; the One Love Energy that encompasses everyone and everything in existence. In its essential nature it is unchanging and eternal. It lives in the lotus of the heart of every being as the Atman, the Divine Witness Consciousness. The Brahman is the Tao of Taoism, the Force of Star Wars, the One Mind of Buddhism, the Holy Spirit of Jesus Christ, the Great Spirit within all things of the Great Mystery. It is the all-pervading Soul and Spirit of the Universe from which all created things emerge and to which they return. Light particles emanate from the Radiance, take forms, and then return to the Radiance. The Supreme Soul or Supreme Spirit. (Note: there is a difference between the meanings of Brahma and Brahman.)

Creatures ~ Sometimes refers to all animals, including the human animals. Depending on context may refer only to the non- human animals. See Animals.

Darshan ~ The vision and blessings of a deity or holy person.

Devas ~ Beings of Light; Celestial Beings; Gods and Goddesses. (Deva is masculine and Devi is feminine.)

Dharma ~ Right conduct; following one's duty or nature; Cosmic Order and Harmony.

Dharmic ~ Of right conduct.

Durga Ma ~ The tender but fierce aspect of Parvati Devi, who slays the demons of the mind.

Ego ~ A person's sense of self-identity; the parts of a person's personality which cover up their true essence.

Gandharvas ~ Celestial singers and musicians.

Gandhi-ji ~ Mohandas K. Gandhi (1869-1948), the Great Soul (Mahatma) who led the Indian independence movement against British rule. He dearly loved the Tulsidas Ramayana; he practiced ahimsa; and when he was shot in the chest, his dying words were "He Rama."

Ganesha ~ Elephant-headed God of Wisdom who removes all obstacles. Son of Lord Shiva and Goddess Parvati.

Guru ~ Literally means "The one who brings you from darkness (gu) to light (ru)." ~ A spiritual teacher, within or without, who imparts wisdom.

Hanuman ~ The Mighty Superhero of the Ramayana: the Supreme Bhakta (Devotee) of Rama and Sita. Extremely intelligent, he possesses the qualities of Strength, Positive Energies, Courage, and Wisdom. His many virtues are extolled in the Hanuman Chalisa, a prayer of forty verses written in an old dialect of Hindi by Saint Tulsidas.

Hara ~ A Name of Lord Shiva.

Hari ~ A Name of Lord Vishnu.

Indra ~ The Vedic Thunder God; King of the gods and goddesses.

Jaya Hanuman! ~ Victory to Hanuman! ~ Jaya means "Victory to" and it also means "Hail to" and "Glory to."

Jaya Shiva Shankara! ~ Victory to Lord Shiva! (Shankara is a Name of Shiva that means Giver of Peace and Happiness.)

Jaya Sita~Rama! ~ Victory to Sita and Rama!

Kali Ma ~ The fierce aspect of Goddess Parvati, who helps people cut through the illusions of their egos.

Kali Yuga ~ The fourth of four ages in the Hindu religion. It is the current age we are living in, the dark iron age when vices are increasing and virtues are on the decline. (A yuga is an epoch or era within a four-age cycle of time.)

Karmas ~ Actions and the results of actions.

Lakshmi Devi ~ The Goddess of Wealth, Beauty, Fortune, Health, Vitality, and Power. Consort of Lord Vishnu.

Lilas ~ Divine Plays or Sports of God.

Lokas ~ Worlds or spheres.

Ma ~ A term of respect, meaning Mother.

Maha~Lakshmi ~ The Divine Feminine Aspect of the Radiant Supreme Reality. Maha~Vishnu's Creative Potency.

Maha~Vishnu ~ The Divine Masculine Aspect of the Radiant Supreme Reality. Maha~Lakshmi's Substratum.

Mahadeva ~ A Name of Lord Shiva, meaning Great God.

Mala ~ A rosary with 108 beads, typically made of a sacred substance, such as sandalwood or rudraksha berries. Used for counting during the spiritual practice of mantra japa, the repetition of a mantra.

Mantras ~ Sacred syllables, words, or phrases. When repeated with concentration, mantras help to calm the mind and open the heart.

Munis ~ Sages, saints, or hermits.

Nagas ~ Semi-divine serpents who dwell in a magical kingdom in the underworld.

Narayana ~ A Name of Lord Vishnu.

Om ~ The original sacred sound. The supreme primordial syllable that ever vibrates through everything in the universes. Om is said to represent the Supreme Spirit, the Brahman.

Om Namah Shivaya ~ A very popular mantra said to bestow both spiritual protection and material prosperity. Literally it means, "I bow to Shiva who is Pure Consciousness and Bliss. I bow to my innermost Self, which is Pure Consciousness and Bliss." When spoken as a greeting, it essentially means "Namaste" or "I honor the Pure Divine Consciousness within you, that is also within me."

Om Shree Hanumate Namaha ~ Powerful mantra to be relieved from troubles by Lord Hanuman. Literally means "I bow to Shree Hanuman, who gives love, strength, devotion, wisdom, and positive energy."

Parvati Devi ~ The Goddess of Love, Devotion, Fertility, Intelligence, Divine Strength, and Power. Consort of Lord Shiva.

Puja ~ Worship.

Puranas ~ Ancient sacred Hindu literature, myths, and legends.

Radiant Supreme Reality ~ See Brahman.

Raghu ~ The great grandfather of Rama. One of the famed kings of the Solar Dynasty.

Rakshasas ~ Demons, ruled by the domineering Ravana.

Rama ~ The Primary Superhero of the Ramayana, who embodies all virtues. He is the embodiment of Goodness: he incarnates to work for the good of the world. He is an Avatar of Maha~Vishnu and the husband of Sita.

Ramabhaktas ~ Devotees of Lord Rama.

Rama~Sita~Rajya ~ The reign of Rama and Sita. In past Ramayanas it was referred to as Rama~Rajya.

Ravana ~ The king of demons who nurtured his vices and dominated the worlds from his city on Lanka island.

Rikshas ~ Bears, led by the wise old Bear King, Jambavan.

Rishis ~ Sages and seers.

Rudra ~ The fierce aspect of Lord Shiva. Hanuman is an Avatar of the eleventh expansion of the Shakti (Power) of Rudra.

Sadhana ~ Spiritual practices that lead to union with the Brahman.

Samadhi ~ An advanced state of meditation in which one is merged in union with the Brahman, the Supreme Spirit.

Samsara ~ Cycles of living in the worldly material realm.

Samskaras ~ Subconscious impressions that are left in the mind by each action.

Sannyasa ~ The life stage of renunciation: renouncing the worldly life and focusing on the spiritual life.

Sannyasi (male), Sannyasini (female) ~ A spiritual renunciate.

Sanskrit ~ Ancient classical language of India. Many Hindu scriptures are written in Sanskrit.

Saraswati Devi ~ The Goddess of Knowledge, Music, Creative Arts, Learning, Writing, and Speech. Consort of Lord Brahma.

Shakahara ~ Vegetarianism based on Ahimsa, the doctrine of doing no harm. In this Ramayana, Shakahara means eating a **vegan** diet in which one does not consume any animal products at all. (Shaka means vegetable and Ahara means to consume or to eat.)

Shakahari (male), Shakaharini (female) ~ One following the Shakahara vegan diet.

Shakti ~ The Divine Feminine Creative Power of the Universes.

Shanti ~ Peace.

Shastras ~ Hindu scriptures.

Shiva ~ The destroyer aspect of the Hindu Trinity. (Maha~Vishnu divides his Supreme Energy into the trinity of Brahma, Vishnu, and Shiva, for the functioning of the universes.) Shiva's consort is Parvati Devi and she takes the forms of Durga Ma and Kali Ma.

Shivabhaktas ~ Devotees of Lord Shiva.

Shivam ~ Auspiciousness or Godliness.

Shivoham ~ Literally means "I Am Shiva" = "I Am God." This mantra acknowledges the Brahman within, just as Jesus Christ taught that "the Kingdom of God is within."

Shri~Pala ~ Shri means Goddess of Wealth and Pala means fruit, so the literal meaning is fruit of Goddess Lakshmi. Includes coconuts and bananas, two highly revered fruits in India.

Shri Rama Jaya Rama Jaya Jaya Rama ~ Potent sacred thirteen-syllabled mantra meaning glory and victory to Rama.

Sita Ma ~ The wife of Sri Rama and the Mother of All the Worlds. She is an Avatar of Maha~Lakshmi, and thus she embodies the Supreme Compassion of the Primordial Shakti.

Solar Dynasty ~ The ancient royal lineage of Lord Rama.

StarFire ~ The source of energy for the Sun and for all of life. It is generated in the core of the Sun, and then radiates out to give energy to all the stars and to all the beings in all the realms. It is the highest healing Love Energy, also called Maha~Vishnu, Brahman, and the Radiant Supreme Reality.

StarFire Radiant Healing Energies of Lord Shiva ~ The highest healing Love Energies that anyone can invoke for healing. These energies can be used to heal oneself, and they can be channeled and transmitted to assist others in healing themselves. Note that "healing" does not necessarily mean "curing." Healing energies can correct imbalances, but if it is the person's time to die, then the healing energies may simply bring acceptance and peace.

Sundara Kandam ~ "The Book of Beauty" ~ Book Five of the Ramayana is the most auspicious book. It brings hope to all who hear it, for in the Sundara Kandam, Hanuman finds Sita. (Sundara means Beauty and Kandam means Book.)

Supreme Being ~ See Brahman.

Surya ~ The Vedic Sun God. The original ancestor of the kings of Sri Rama's solar lineage.

Treta Yuga ~ The second of four ages in the Hindu religion. (A yuga is an epoch or era within a four-age cycle of time.) Past Ramayanas took place in the Treta Yuga, but this version happened in the Kali Yuga.

Tulsidas ~ Goswami Tulasidasa (1532-1623), a poet-saint of India, who wrote *Shri Ramacharitamanasa: The Holy Lake of the Acts of Rama*. He is said to be an incarnation of the first poet to compose the Ramayana, the revered Sage Valmiki.

Upanishads ~ A series of sacred Sanskrit texts that are part of the Vedas. They contain the wisdom of India's ancient mystics.

Vaikunta ~ The celestial abode of Lord Vishnu and Goddess Lakshmi.

Valmiki ~ The first poet-saint to compose the Ramayana in India. (His revered version is dated variously from the fifth century BCE to the first century BCE.)

Vanaras ~ A race of magical divine monkeys who assist Rama in the Ramayana. Their kings are Sugriva and Vali, and they live in the enchanted forest kingdom of Kishkindha.

Varuna ~ The Vedic Sea God.

Vasanas ~ Past karmic impressions in the mind and the behavioral tendencies that arise out of those mental imprints.

Vayu ~ The Vedic Wind God.

Vedas ~ The most ancient Hindu scriptures.

Vedic ~ Of the Vedas.

Vegan ~ A diet, philosophy, and lifestyle that is one of the highest expressions of ahimsa, the Vedic principle of doing no harm. Recognizing that it is impossible to be one hundred percent perfectly pure vegan, still a vegan strives to do as little harm as possible. Thus vegans do not eat animal flesh or fluids, like meat, fish, dairy, butter, ghee, eggs, and honey, and they do not wear animal skins, leather, fur, and so on. Vegans also do not support zoos, rodeos, horse races, circuses, lab experimentations, or any other activity that confines and harms living beings. Also, a small group of vegans are beginning to speak out with reasons for compassionately phasing out the pet phenomenon.

Vishnu ~ The protector~sustainer aspect of the Hindu Trinity. (Maha~Vishnu divides his Supreme Energy into the trinity of Brahma, Vishnu, and Shiva, for the functioning of the universes.) Vishnu's consort is Lakshmi Devi.

Yogi (male), Yogini (female) ~ One who practices Yogic sadhana, which includes the practices of meditation, chanting, repetition of mantras, studying the scriptures, serving others, and performing asanas (body postures). The yogi or yogini does any or all of these daily spiritual practices with the goal of attaining the highest state of union (Yoga) with the Brahman, the Supreme Spirit within and without.

Bibliography

Ackerman, Jennifer. *The Genius of Birds*. Penguin Books, New York, 2016.

Arundale, G.S. *Kundalini: An Occult Experience*. The Theosophical Publishing House, Madras, India, 1938.

Bekoff, Marc. *The Emotional Lives of Animals: A Leading Scientist Explores Animal Joy, Sorrow, and Empathy — and Why They Matter*. New World Library, California, 2007.

Bhushan, Bharat. *Birds of Ramayana*. Vishwakarma Publications, Mumbai, India, 2016.

Buck, William. *Ramayana*. University of California Press, California & England, 1976.

Carman, Judy. *Peace to All Beings: Veggie Soup for the Chicken's Soul*. Lantern Books, New York, 2003.

Carman, Judy and Tina Volpe. *The Missing Peace: The Hidden Power of Our Kinship with Animals*. Dreamriver Press, Pennsylvania, 2009.

Das, Bhagavan. *It's Here Now (Are You?)*. Broadway Books, New York, 1997.

Frawley, David. *The Oracle of Rama* (cards and companion guide). Mandala Publishing, California, 2005.

Gandhi, Mohandas K. *Book of Prayers*. Berkeley Hills Books, California, 1999.

Gray, J.E.B. *Tales from India*. Oxford University Press, Great Britain, 1961.

Gurudev Siddha Peeth. *Does Death Really Exist?* By Swami Muktananda. SYDA Foundation, New York, 1981.

Harper San Francisco, Staff. *Peace Prayers: Meditations, Affirmations, Invocations, Poems, and Prayers for Peace.* Harper San Francisco of Harper Collins Publishers, New York, 1992.

Hoff, Benjamin. *The Te of Piglet.* Penguin Books, New York, 1992.

House of Nightingale. *Hanuman Chalisa.* Unknown author, unknown date.

Hughes, Serge. *The Little Flowers of St. Francis: And Other Franciscan Writings.* Mentor-Omega, The New American Library, New York, 1964.

Keshavadas, Sadguru Sant. *Saints of India.* Temple of Cosmic Religion, Washington, D.C., 1975.

Mack, John. *Passport to the Cosmos: Human Transformation and Alien Encounters.* White Crow Books, United Kingdom, 2011. (First published 1999.)

Masson, Jeffrey and Susan McCarthy. *When Elephants Weep: The Emotional Lives of Animals.* Delta, Dell Publishing, New York, 1995.

Menon, Ramesh. *The Ramayana: A Modern Retelling of the Great Indian Epic.* North Point Press, New York, 2001.

Muktananda, Swami. *Meditate.* State University of New York Press, New York, 1980, 1991.

Narayan, R.K. *The Ramayana: A Shortened Modern Prose Version of the Indian Epic (Suggested by the Tamil Version of Kamban).* Penguin Books, U.S.A., 2006. (First published 1972.)

Nhat Hanh, Thich. *Living Buddha, Living Christ*. Riverhead Books, New York, 1995.

Nhat Hanh, Thich. *Peace Is Every Step: The Path of Mindfulness in Everyday Life*. Bantam Books, New York, 1991.

Nhat Hanh, Thich. *The Energy of Prayer: How to Deepen Your Spiritual Practice*. Parallax Press, California, 2006.

Pai, Anant. *Rama* (comic book). India Book House Ltd., Bombay, India, 1995.

Pattanaik, Devdutt. *my Hanuman Chalisa*. Rupa Publications, New Delhi, India, 2017.

Pattanaik, Devdutt. *Sita: An Illustrated Retelling of the Ramayana*. Penguin Books, India, 2013.

Prime, Ranchor. *Ramayana: A Tale of Gods and Demons*. Mandala Publishing, California, 2001, 2004.

Raghaveshananda, Swami. *Pictorial Ramayana*. Art: Padmavasan. Adhyaksha, Sri Ramakrishna Math, Chennai, India, 1988.

Rajagopalachari, C. *Ramayana*. Bharatiya Vidya Bhavan, Bombay, India, 1962.

Ramanujan, A.K. Essay: *Three Hundred Ramayanas: Five Examples and Three Thoughts on Translation*. 1987

Rampuri, Baba. *Baba: Autobiography of a Blue-Eyed Yogi*. Bell Tower, New York, 2005.

Roberts, Elizabeth and Elias Amidon. *Earth Prayers From Around the World: 365 Prayers, Poems, and Invocations for Honoring the Earth*. Harper San Francisco of Harper Collins Publishers, New York, 1991.

Sivananda Ashram. *Kirtan: Sivananda Chant Book.* Unknown author, publisher, date.

Sivananda, Swami. *Essence of Ramayana.* The Divine Life Society, Himalayas, India, 1996.

Sri Ramakrishna Math. *Adhyatma Ramayana: The Spiritual Version of the Rama Saga.* Translated by Swami Tapasyananda. Sri Ramakrishna Math, Chennai, India, 1988.

Subramaniam, Kamala. *Ramayana.* Bharatiya Vidya Bhavan, Mumbai, India, 1981.

Tulasidasa. *Shriramacharitamanasa (The Holy Lake of the Acts of Rama).* Edited and Translated into Hindi and English by R.C. Prasad. Motilal Banarsidass Publishers, India, 1990.

Vanamali. *The Song of Rama: Visions of the Ramayana.* Blue Dove Press, California, 2001.

Vedanta Society of Southern California. *Shankara's Crest-Jewel of Discrimination (Viveka-Chudamani).* Translated with an Introduction to Shankara's Philosophy, by Swami Prabhavananda and Christopher Isherwood. Vedanta Press, California, 1947.

Vedanta Society of Southern Califorgna. *The Upanishads: Breath of Eternal Life.* Translated by Swami Prabhavananda and Frederick Manchester. Signet Classics, U.S.A., 2002. (First published 1948.)

Acknowledgements

Firstly, here is the context for my gratefulness: in 2019 my chronic health issues worsened (forcing me into early retirement), and then on January 25, 2020 my Dad died suddenly at seventy-seven (after heart surgery) leaving my Mom and me alone to quarantine together through the virus pandemic. All of those misfortunes required me to shrink my world. I am incredibly grateful to the small group of "safe people" who encouraged me to keep going through all the difficulties.

My Mom is the star of this gratitude list. Thank you, Mom, for all of your love, support, sustaining songs, hugs, shelter, and fantastic vegan meals. We are blessed in our little wild green urban forest realm. I loved writing this book from my tree-house temple... my colorful sanctuary that Dad referred to as the bird's nest! (Thank you, Dad, wherever you are, for always supporting my writing.)

Deep gratitude also goes to my two bright adorable sons, Zak and Gabriel; and to their kind generous Papa, Ken; and to their wonderful older brother Sam; and to Ken's sweet sister, Shirel. Thank you, Shirel, the big sister I always dreamed of, for being there for me in so many ways. I love you dearly.

Thanks also to my beautiful and thoughtful brother, Adam, and to all my family and friends. I really appreciate all the love.

I am grateful to my beloved Grandparents and to all of my ancestors, of blood and of spirit. I bow to all the many teachers whom I have been blessed to know and study.

Lastly, but certainly not least-ly, thank you Shankar Narayan for inspiring me to confidently use the "vegan" word. Your Sthitaprajna Vegan Forest is a unique refuge in this world. (**www.vgan.in**) Thank you for all of your good works for the animals as the Founder President of Satvik Vegan Society (formerly Indian Vegan Society). I am so thrilled to be a contributing author for your forthcoming book, *Satva — 2001-2021: Chronicling 20 Years of Vegan Journey*.

May all beings be blessed with love and compassion.
Om Namah Shivaya.

About the Author

Tejaswini Shankara, who goes by Teja (pronounced "Tay-juh"), is a yogini-mystic of the Shakahara StarFire Tribe, a Ramayana scholar, a Mama of two amazing young men, and a barefoot nature lover who loves the Sun, orange marigolds, sunflowers, red roses, trees, birds, stars, red rocks, hot black coffee (organic, fair trade, dark roast!), pinecones, amethyst crystals, sacred science fiction/fantasy realms, and the vision of Hanuman in the pine tree forests, ever ringing his bells and singing "Rama, Rama, Rama!"

As a blended Hindu-Buddhist-Taoist-Jedi (who also bows to Christ Consciousness, Nature-Loving Science, and nature-based traditions like Tibetan Buddhist and Native American), Shakaharini StarFire Teja Ray aspires to send nourishing spiritual energies and love energies out to all beings each day. She is a vegan visionary with various ever-evolving ministries, such as a former blog on which she published thirty vegan articles: starfireteja.wordpress.com/blog/.

At the heart of the Star Wars saga is the Jedi understanding that the Force is in everything and everyone, so the Jedi feel compassion for all living beings. Thus Jedi = Vegan Ahimsa = Shakahara. As a Jedi wannabe, Teja Ray seeks to cultivate that level of superhero compassion in her daily vegan life. And, she visualizes a world in which all the good peaceful people turn the darksiders (like Ravana) back to the Light!

Learning to embrace early retirement, Teja Ray writes for the animals in her tree-house temple over a small green urban forest. Perhaps someday others will join her Shakahara StarFire Tribe.

VeganRamayana.mystrikingly.com